The Dance That Makes You Vanish

DIFFERENCE INCORPORATED
Roderick A. Ferguson and Grace Kyungwon Hong, series editors

THE DANCE THAT MAKES YOU VANISH

Cultural Reconstruction in
Post-Genocide Indonesia

RACHMI DIYAH LARASATI

Difference Incorporated

University of Minnesota Press
Minneapolis
London

Published by the University of Minnesota Press
111 Third Avenue South, Suite 290
Minneapolis, MN 55401-2520
http://www.upress.umn.edu

Library of Congress Cataloging-in-Publication Data

Larasati, Rachmi Diyah.
    The dance that makes you vanish : cultural reconstruction in post-genocide
Indonesia / Rachmi Diyah Larasati.
        (Difference incorporated)
    Includes bibliographical references and index.
    ISBN 978-0-8166-7993-5 (hc : alk. paper)
    ISBN 978-0-8166-7994-2 (pb : alk. paper)
    1. Dance—Government policy—Indonesia. 2. Dance—Social
aspects—Indonesia. 3. Women dancers—Indonesia. 4. Collective
memory—Indonesia. 5. Indonesia—History—Coup d'état, 1965—Social
aspects. 6. Indonesia—Politics and government—1966–1998. 7. Indonesia—
Cultural policy. I. Title. II. Series: Difference incorporated.
    GV1703.I53L37 2013
    793.3'19598—dc23

                                                            2012041448

Printed in the United States of America on acid-free paper

The University of Minnesota is an equal-opportunity educator and employer.

20 19 18 17 16 15 14 13   10 9 8 7 6 5 4 3 2 1

For my grandmother Siti Samidjah,
the disappeared parents and relatives,
and the children of the many who died without
ceremonies in 1965 and the years that followed

CONTENTS

ACKNOWLEDGMENTS

This book has been a long time in coming and would not have been possible without the support of the community of Indonesian scholars and activists, feminist scholars, and former political prisoners in Indonesia: many invisible bodies—in particular, members of the women's movement in Indonesia—who have been forgotten or dishonored, or whose bodies disappeared into mass graves. To the former political prisoners arrested during and after 1965, for their support, friendship, and generosity in sharing their experiences, I am profoundly indebted. I also thank the many children of those who disappeared in 1965 and the years that followed, whose longing for a real "home," not unlike my own, has inspired the possibility of remembering.

In this book, I trace how the female dancing bodies obedient to the state's agenda are able to attain mobility while simultaneously erasing the unruly bodies that are not. I focus on the issues surrounding the widespread Indonesian massacres in 1965 and the years that followed. This book commences with my memories of dancing as a child, the dancing that later granted me access to the world of *Pegawai Negeri* (Indonesian civil servants) and travel abroad.

The writing and publication of this book would not have been possible without support from Grace Hong, Roderick Ferguson, and Richard Morrison from the University of Minnesota Press. Nor would it have been possible without the guidance and support of my grandmother Siti Samidjah and my mentors Geoffrey Robinson, Marta Savigliano, Michael Ross (UCLA), and Henk Maier (UC-Riverside), as well as, Susan Foster, Susan Rose, Anna Scott, Priya Srinivasan, and Linda Tomko. Philip Yampolsky from the Ford Foundation made possible my returns to the United States and to the PhD program that granted broader access to certain kinds of critical thinking about my own and others' practice of dance. The writing of this book was made possible with support from the following awards and grants: Institute for Advanced Studies, Grant in Aid, Imagine Fund (University of Minnesota); the Ford Foundation (International Fellowship, 2001–4); American Association of University Women (AAUW) for International Fellowship (2001); the Home Country Project (2004); Asian Scholarship Foundation/Ford Foundation (2002–3); Lemelson Visiting Scholar/UCLA CSEAS 2006–7. I thank the family of Ted and Helen Kinan, the Indonesian Embassy representatives in Phnom Penh, and the Royal University of Fine Arts for their generous support.

Many individuals lent support in a variety of important and unforgettable ways during my research: Julie Chenot (UNESCO, Cambodia, 2002), François Giovalluchi (AFD, Phnom Penh, 2002), Matthew Brensilver, Princess Buphadevi Sihanouk, Jaime Sarte, Pedro Soares Brinca, João Pedro Gomes, Miguel Angel del Arco Blanco, Leslie Dwyer, Degung Santikarma, Gung Alit, Ibu Mayun, Mohsin Alam Bhatt, Dr. Gregorius Subanar and Dr. Baskara Wardaya from PUSDEP, and the graduate program at Sanata Dharma University, Gus Dur and Syarikat Indonesia, Termana and the family of *Taman 65* Bali, the French Cultural Center in Yogyakarta, Maria Hartiningsih (Kompas), Gung Ayu, Gung Tri, Rita Dharani, Matthew Isaac Cohen, Alit Ambara, Lillian Wu, Koes Yuliadi, Y. Subowo, Utik S, Rina M, Erlina PS, Heni W, and Bambang Pudjasworo.

Upon my arrival at the University of Minnesota, I received a warm welcome and continual support from the dance program and the Department of Theatre Arts and Dance, Michal Kobialka, Ananya Chatterjea, Carl Flink, Toni Pierce, Dominic Taylor, Sonja Kuftinec, and Nora Jenneman; and a community of mentorship from Roderick Ferguson, Jigna Desai, Richa Nagar, Abdi Samatar, and David Pellow. I am grateful for the institutional support I have received in Minnesota from Ann Waltner and Susannah Smith (IAS). I am thankful for the friendship of Hakim Abderrezak, Giancarlo Casale, Sumanth Gopinath, Mohannad Ghawanmeh, Bret Wilson, Matt Rahaim, Ali Momeni, Himadeep Muppidi, M. Bianet Castellanos, David Karjannen, Teri Caraway, Michael Goldman, Cawo Abdi, Keli Garrett, Uri Sands, Gayani Sriwardena, Reem El Radi, Fatimah Zahra, Leila Bonini, and Fiza Jaafar-Tribbett, and the community of graduate students: Rita Kompelmakher, Virgil Slade, Pham Nhu Quynh, Maria Jose, Joya John, Alperen Evrin. Finally, I thank Dag Yngvesson (in whom I place the precious trust of understanding my "(post)colonial anxiety") and Barbara Yngvesson for their valuable editorial comments and continual encouragement, the Yngvesson family for their support, and Aji and family in Drupadi.

INTRODUCTION

Dancing on the Mass Grave

Many women gather in the yard in front of my house each evening while children play and practice certain dance.[1] Every day they inhabit a kind of "no man's land." Except there is a man who hides his gun in his bedroom, who comes and goes to the Air Force base surrounded by sugar cane, in East Java. His body has the wounds of war, seven in total. Holes and strange marks cover his skin. His name is Mr. Soek. Those holes are deep, cutting his flesh and marking his skin weirdly because of their itchiness. My finger often wants to caress those holes, and I once was able to enter one of them to touch the scarred tissue that had replaced the skin at the bullet's entry point. I often ask him about the cause of those injuries. He forbids me to keep looking at the scars, and furthermore to keep asking him what was the cause of those injuries. Many people told me that he is sakti, *possessing divine power, because he is still alive although many bullets entered him. For me he was* sakti *also, not because of his wounded body, but because of his signature on a piece of paper, which enabled me to be admitted to a school. Because of Mr. Soek, I could go to school, although I had to leave my childhood friends behind. They did not get the signature because many of their parents were missing and they failed to submit proper letters from the government about their "clean identity."[2] Mr. Soek was like a magician. When I needed a new school, his name suddenly became the name of my father, and he came to school wearing his Air Force uniform and introduced himself as my parent. He was the only man in the house where I stayed.*[3] *One day he told me that his first and second wounds were from the fight for independence; the rest were from the civil war in Madiun. He explained that he was not sure who shot him. In one of his missions he was facing many women in Javanese sarongs, running around. It was confusing for him. He didn't know if they were a rebel group or just innocent civilians. He made the decision not to shoot them, but suddenly from behind there was gunfire and many bullets flew at him. He did not have a chance to see where those bullets came from. He was very young and in the middle of a teak forest in Madiun, East Java, in 1948.*

I was never able to retrieve his memory and his unspoken witness in detail, including whether he killed the people who resided in the teak forest, who, to my knowledge, were mostly farmers. Perhaps before I was old enough to be trusted with such information, a loaded truck of Army men came to the neighborhood and found me on the street playing with neighbors, singing and dancing in a circle, pretending to be a dance teacher. The leader of the Army asked if we, the children who were playing on the street, knew where Mr. Soek's house was. All the children were pointing at me. I walked slowly in front of them, bringing the soldiers to my home. Mr. Soek was in the corner of the house, standing up straight like in the photographs of Air Force training that I often saw in magazines, yet his body was shaking. A month after that, I realized Mr. Soek did not wear his uniform anymore; he had been forced to resign his position because the office discovered his connection to the family of the dancer in our house, and that was forbidden. He was married (illegally) to a female dancer, who was accused of being a former Gerwani member. Gerwani (Gerakan Wanita Indonesia) was a women's movement during the time of Sukarno, the first president of Indonesia. Although the group was legal under Sukarno, later, during the rule of Suharto (the second president), it was blamed for allegedly sympathizing with the communists and was banned and persecuted. During and after the time when Suharto came to power, many members of Gerwani simply disappeared.[4]

Membership in Gerwani became a monster of motherhood in my house. For me, "Gerwani women" were my aunties, dance teachers, neighbors, and the parents of many of my friends. Yet for Mr. Soek, my aunt, the woman he loved, and whose family he had knowingly protected with the strength of his name, position, and "clean" status, had caused his uniform and good standing, in effect his entire life, to be suddenly and violently revoked. For the remaining fifteen years before he died, I felt he was never quite himself again.

At the house of the head of the village a few years after Mr. Soek's arrest, I saw a program on television about "Gerwani women." Confronted with the gap between enforced state discourse and the familiarity of my own family, the words themselves began to sound strange: ominous, but not in the direct, literal sense promoted by the government. Instead they formed an uneasy, ill-defined space around my memories of women, my women, and their dancing. The knowledge of our own families was surrounded by the reconstructed unfamiliarity of violence that sought to re-narrativize our own experience. Unable to avoid it, in spite of my fear I began quietly mapping each encounter with the narratives of Gerwani and of women, moving, discussing, thinking, or "plotting." We danced and grew up with the unspoken struggle of memory ever present in our own households.

In some sense, this book is a response to the experiences of my childhood and of my later life as a performer and young scholar, as infused with my inheritance of both a powerful dance practice and a well-hidden yet horrifying political identity. As I attempt to theorize my own history and that of the millions of others who were targeted and persecuted or killed by the "New Order" regime, the state's narrative use of the female dancing body as a symbol of great power, albeit often an "evil" power, becomes a point of departure to discuss the theorization of bodily mimesis in relation to historical context, as discussed by Edward Said in *The World, the Text, and the Critic*.[5]

Following Said, in my book, the creation of "text" refers to expression through writing, bodily representation, or other media as a methodologically conscious reconstruction of identity. Here it is used as an attempt to interrogate the official unquestionable-ness of a ubiquitous, hegemonic, and mythical text: Indonesian national reality as produced by the military and state in collusion with the forces that determine global political, economic, and artistic alliances. Yet my writing is in many ways a paradox, indebted to and enabled by the very texts and forces it confronts with all the strength I can muster. In this context, I engage with the process of subject formation, the creation of "self" that, under pressure from the external forces of myth, is affected by dominant narratives that vie to replace embodied memory, even, and particularly, within the private space of family and household. The concept of myth, however, which is often understood to be the source of "primitive" ritualistic behavior in groups of humans outside of our own, is in this context critically expanded. Here, myth also follows the modern practice of ritualistic violence and functions to categorize certain unwanted bodies from within our own ranks as Other, as belonging to a group whose alleged actions threaten the very foundations of what we must think of as "ours."

Mimesis in this context is a creation of text that simultaneously departs from and resembles the particularities of Indonesian history, the weaving of a complex fabric of myth and experience. The resulting cloth appears as a continuous and unedited whole, yet is riddled with gaps through which millions of actual bodies have both physically vanished and been mythologically expelled. These real, vanished bodies are then replaced with simulacra that cover the holes left behind; in my writing, I use the word *replica* to make this connection. Replication occurs as new, historically, politically "clean" dancers are employed to absorb and embody the practices of artists targeted by the state, recreating the image of corporeality in the traditions of those who no longer officially exist. The vanished dancers and their families, and those women put in prison or left at home but stripped of their practice, serve as the point of departure for my choreography of theory in this manuscript. While ethnographic research and oral history are tools I use to recapture memories and interpretations of those events, the narratives and embodied experiences I gather surround me, intertwining with the texts, and the corporeality of oppression that I must revisit. I combine my memory, corporeal experience, and interpretations to craft my own historical representation, in the form of a book, attempting a structural resistance through the precise mapping of forced political relocations and dislocations enacted by the New Order and simultaneously hidden within the discourse of a "natural" reaction to a universalized framework of good and evil.

This book is also based on my experiences growing up and making my way through the national educational system during the Suharto era. In the classroom, I learned that Suharto, the second president of Indonesia, was a national hero. At school, I was repeatedly taught that on many different occasions, such as in 1965 and during the Madiun clash, the Indonesian Communist Party (Partai Komunis Indonesia or PKI) was responsible for the murder of Army generals and high-ranking officers. The PKI, then, was to be seen as a group that had betrayed the nation's strength and thus constituted a threat to our national unity and security. Therefore, every citizen had an obligation to involve himself or herself in opposing communism and in taking certain precautions against the perceived threat of its continued spread.

My schooling, however, never enabled me to learn the fate or whereabouts of my neighbor's mother, or my dance teachers, my grandfather, or all of the men and women by whom I had been surrounded who disappeared one by one and never returned. Some of the women who were left always sat in the front yard and never mentioned anything related to these disappearances. Every two weeks most women went to the military district office, leaving early in the morning and coming back after dark. I did not understand what they were doing and why they always went there, except that they all seemed very nervous and tried to put their corsets on very tightly, just like when my friends and I put on our costumes before dancing *Gandrung* and *Tari Bondan,* two dances in the Javanese style practiced by women. Although my teacher always told me that each dance consisted of different values and class markers, I danced them both enthusiastically.

Retracing First Performances:
The Genealogy of Reappearances and Erasure

It was the middle of the 1970s, the day of my first performance, my feet stepping on the pot made of clay and lightly dancing above it, my right hand holding an umbrella. A teacher had told me that I should imagine "travel" and "optimism," but in an elegant way, when performing those movements. Although too young to understand what she meant, I would soon be traveling to different regions across the country, and a few short years after that I would begin to perform abroad. Slowly, as I became more practiced in the forms required for official dancers, I began to forget about the people I knew who had disappeared. I was busy practicing and rehearsing for my many performances in villages, for television or government offices on Independence Day, and always on October 1, when the Army celebrates *Kesaktian Pancasila*. This day, commemorating the sacred power of *Pancasila* (the five principles of Indonesian state ideology endlessly drummed into the minds of the citizenry by every teacher and government officer) was the day in 1965 when attacks, allegedly by Communist Party members, were dispelled by both troops and civilians allied with then-general Suharto. Yet of course the commemoration, based around the events of a single day, does not remind us of the hundreds of thousands of accused "communists" who lost their lives at the hands of the military shortly afterward. In connection with the many artists and dancers who were targeted and disappeared during and after these attacks, I take the state's imaginative transformation of a day, September 30, into the ultimate national "zero hour"—during which our country was said to be saved from destruction and born anew—as a point of departure for my argument on amnesia and remembering.

As an important condition of possibility for such an argument, and to some extent for this entire book, I reflect further on my inclusion in the "clean" household of an Air Force family. This move, while itself traumatic, finally enabled me to reconfigure my alienation from the social and political mainstream. This thorny gift of acceptability in the eyes of the state, for which a number of grave sacrifices were made, has ultimately provided me with greater access to the dis-familiarity and disconnects within my own memories, and by historical/theoretical extension, those of the many, many others less "lucky" than myself.

From within the relative safety and obscurity of my grandmother's yard, where I learned to dance, my life began to change quickly and permanently. I rarely looked back, as new alliances were formed and old ones erased and forgotten. After performing nationally for a few years as a teenager, one day I was told to undergo a *skrening* (screening), after which I received a kind of agreement letter to become a government employee of Indonesia. During the *skrening* I was asked to make a diagram of my family tree, to see if there were any sort of connections to the Communist Party in my family; even a distant relative known to have been in an "affiliated" organization would have disqualified, and probably blacklisted me, or far worse. This was my final test, and with the *sakti*-ness of Mr. Soek's signature, my "dirty" genealogy was officially made invisible, obscuring my connection to a disappeared grandfather and many other "subversive" relatives. Soon afterward, I was inducted as a member of the civil service and began teaching at the Indonesian state Institute of the Arts (ISI), in Yogyakarta, where President Suharto, the person mainly responsible for the killings in 1965 and the "antisubversive" policies that followed, visited in 1984 for the opening ceremony. By that time I had become a member of the Indonesian Cultural Mission, an official, state-sanctioned dance troupe whose function was to promote Indonesia's national identity abroad. Thus, drawing on my experience as a dancer, civil servant, and national cultural representative, and my transformation from a so-called unruly, unwanted body, I look at the study of travel and mobility, of "feminist" resistance and co-optation from a dislocated perspective that might approximate that of Said's worldly exile.

During one such cultural mission in 1994, in the corner of a library in Europe, I found a picture from 1973 of dancers who were identified as Indonesian "political prisoners." Recognizing the style and location as close to home, I moved closer, thinking I might pick out some familiar faces; instead, I found something that made me begin to question aspects of my education, particularly much of the history I had learned in school along with my fellow Indonesian citizens over the past few decades. Three years later, in 1997, while studying with a former staff member of the Amnesty London headquarters at UCLA, I was suddenly struck by an awful realization, as I was flooded again with the memories of my neighbors, many of them dancers like myself and my family, who had disappeared and never returned. Thousands of miles from home in an English-speaking classroom, my sense of historical identification was radically re-oriented, as I read that in 1965, more than a million Indonesians were killed and thousands more imprisoned without trial on isolated islands. When I returned to Indonesia in 1998, with much of the "common sense" I had developed as a child and young woman altered or lost, I began to ask questions. Many people were shocked that I would even speak of such matters, others told their stories and versions of events excitedly, and others, still, simply refused to respond or react in any way at all.

Later that year, driven by these questions and seduced by the opportunity to obtain an international degree, I accepted an invitation to go back to UCLA as a master's candidate in world arts and cultures. However, even there I found it difficult to free myself from the constraints of being known as a dancer, and therefore associated with the context of official Indonesian culture missions and expected to report on issues of traditional art, which are assumed by many Western scholars to be completely unrelated to politics. (For me, such intellectual positions appear eerily similar to those of the Indonesian state itself.) Furthermore, in the year 2000 I stood trial in Yogyakarta, accused of "victimizing" my then-husband by leaving him behind at home during my schooling abroad, which was considered shocking and inappropriate behavior, especially for a female dancer and civil servant. As a result, the process of gaining a Western education became a geopolitical negotiation of the location of rights: I gained crucial access to a new perspective on my nation's history,[6] yet I lost my rights to my own house and with it many highly personal belongings associated with my history, including several of Mr. Soek's letters to me while I was completing my undergraduate education.

Drawing on this experience, I discuss the interconnectedness of state patriarchy, citizenship, and mobility in the context of the (inter) nationalized female dancing body. Must the fleeting promise of feminist resistance contained within global mobility be counterbalanced by slippage and loss of access within the space of the nation? Even as I move on and off far-flung performance spaces and the Western academic stage, I am continually reminded that I am expected to return "home," that I am still "working" for the government (despite my long absence, my attempts to step down from my position as an Indonesian civil servant have been held up at various levels of local and national bureaucracy for more than a decade), and that I must reiterate and reproduce Indonesian culture and obey the requirements of the state as I promised. To this end, I am also well educated: in order to become a civil servant and traveling state performer, I was required to attend several month-long courses entitled *Penataran P4* or "Upgrading Course on the Directives for the Realization and Implementation of Pancasila."[7]

This is, however, also "useful" for the crucial project of historical reflection in the context of this book. From the deeply ingrained experience of learning at the hands of the government, I depart on an analysis of the Indonesian state's emphasis on certain kinds of indoctrination. Further, I examine the ways in which culture, art, and performance are made ideologically inseparable from national history and the politics of memory, the reconstruction of which serves to erase the extreme violence and chaos on which Suharto's New Order state itself was founded. Thus, I trace the history of the female dancing body that vanishes and is then "replaced," its experience and the fact of its disappearance erased from view by new, highly indoctrinated, strictly trained female bodies—not unlike the idealized Indonesian citizen that lives within myself. The art forms once practiced by the vanished dancers, after being reclaimed and ideologically retooled by the state, are considered sufficiently cleansed of the "subversive" aura of those who once mastered and embodied them, and, as such, safe to be included as part of the official concept of national tradition.

A Note on the Ethics of Categorization and Publication

As I began this research and book project, I interviewed people who could be considered victims of recent Indonesian history, as well as those often thought of as perpetrators (both terms are problematic and I apply them sparingly) of the violence in 1965 and the years that followed. In Indonesia, these two categorizations have very different implications and interpretations, depending on where you stand in relation to the events of this period. In the course of my work, I documented people's stories through photographs, as well as occasionally with video and audio recordings. The ethnographic notes in this manuscript mostly reflect my childhood memories and familiarity with the oral histories of the women surrounding me as well as the violence perpetrated against them, including rape, imprisonment, and murder. Because of the continuing political sensitivity of information related to 1965 and the treatment of suspected communists, the stories and impressions I gathered have become elements of an ongoing process of negotiation. At stake are difficult decisions as to which parts of this long journey it is possible to mention specifically or describe in detail in order to support my arguments in this book while minimizing the potential to cause harm or put others at risk.

This research also looks at written reports, magazine articles, and newsletters by Human Rights Watch, documents prepared by Amnesty International, Komnas Perempuan (National Commission on Violence Against Women), and certain nongovernmental organization (NGO) reports. Because of the continuing sensitivity of the issues dealt with in this book, all people involved or who have been interviewed for this text remain anonymous, except those who specifically wished to speak out regarding the Suharto regime and asked that their names be included. To respect them, I follow each person's individual requests. As a consequence, there are some inconsistencies in my approach, especially regarding interviews with specific individuals.

I. TO REMEMBER
DIFFERENTLY

Paradoxical Statehood and Preserved Value

Two hours ago, I performed the Javanese court dance Srimpi. *Like many such dances,* Srimpi *places the female body at its center, attaching to it many ritualistic and often sexualized meanings. The female body as signifier has been used incessantly over the past forty years by the Indonesian government to create its own national cultural identity as a peaceful, perhaps "exotic" place steeped in the traditions of the past. But Indonesia has not always been so peaceful.*

I read these words in a post-performance discussion during a 2005 event at the University of California-Los Angeles (UCLA), one part of a larger celebration of global performance, entitled "WAC [World Arts and Cultures] Is Back." Perhaps, without obvious explanation, I was hoping to capture the urgency of the potential for different cultural narratives in this space (U.S. academia) through the presentation of my paper following the performance. Yet this performance was another example of a replica of Indonesian dance as a cultural text, one that renders a mesmerized aesthetic, one already mediated by pretext: the colonial narrative.[1] Although in the context of "WAC Is Back," the dance was practiced and performed by dancers (myself and another woman) from Indonesia—the independent state formerly colonized by the Dutch—my effort to reconfigure a colonial-era cultural policy that was embraced by the independent state (particularly during the Suharto regime) still strongly functioned to (re)confirm a certain myth issuing from Dutch narratives about a "timeless," sacred dance from Java.

In this context, through my own narrative departures from canonized understandings of Indonesian arts, I hoped my representation of the form might serve to mediate outsider unfamiliarity with the specific, political religiosity of Javanese dance. The aesthetic presentation, however, remained the same. In this sense, the performance project risked the mistranslation of its cultural meaning and context. Also, although the form is located in two different lines, or loci, of cultural representation—one based on the enduring colonial interpretation of the dance and the other in the idea of the performing body as translator of historical text—the current performance space was already steeped in the sustained myth, mediated by the presence of traveling, dancing bodies, which arose as the colonial reports describing these dance genres were first distributed. In this context, both text and movement have served to establish, confirm, and negotiate desire for an imagined native cultural knowledge, particularly in the Western world.[2] The longevity of the concept of the "peaceful Dutch East Indies," now transformed as the peaceful, democratic, independent Indonesian nation-state, remains unchallenged, bolstered by the aesthetic glamorization ubiquitously present on the global stage of "world dance."

Following my performance of the canonical, elegant, royal Javanese form *Srimpi*, I proceeded to explain that in my famously peaceful nation, upward of one million people were killed, disappeared, imprisoned, or exiled in "response" to an odd, poorly organized political action in 1965 that was later claimed to be a failed coup d'état. The Indonesian military, under the leadership of then-general Suharto, quickly seized on the act—and the sketchy, confusing nature of the information surrounding it—changing its title from the self-proclaimed "Gerakan 30 September," or the September 30th Movement, to "Gerakan 30 September PKI," or the September 30th Movement of the Indonesian Communist Party (Partai Komunis Indonesia or PKI). The event was thereafter officially known by the acronym G30S-PKI. The letters PKI, pushed up against those that signify the event itself (G30S), thus constituted the Suharto regime's first production of officialized history, a strategy on which it was to rely heavily in order to keep itself in power for the next thirty years. Disseminated on a national scale so soon after the fact, the foundational abbreviation G30S-PKI supplanted other knowledge of the September 30th movement (including the basic detail that it actually took place on October 1), naturalizing the link between the membership of Partai Komunis Indonesia and the so-called coup and establishing their connection as a key element of the new Indonesian "collective memory."

During the event itself, six Army generals and one high-ranking officer then serving under Indonesia's first president, Sukarno, were murdered by a group of loyalists who claimed to be protecting Sukarno from an impending rightwing coup. Shortly after the event, the largely right-wing Indonesian military alleged that the murders were carried out by members of the PKI, who it, in turn, accused of masterminding an attempted coup d'état (thus, both sides claimed to have acted as the saviors of the ever-popular Sukarno).[3] Based on his own unfounded yet widely publicized assertions, then-general Suharto called for a nationwide state of emergency and the establishment of martial law in response to the impending "communist threat."

In order to "protect" the nation, the army quickly began a wave of killings and arrests lasting several months, targeting anyone suspected or accused of association with the PKI, which until then had been both legal and quite popular. In the ensuing atmosphere of chaos and terror, Suharto and the military used their hurriedly constructed position of authority to maximum advantage, effectively implementing an actual coup d'état, albeit in slow motion: Sukarno's grip on the nation was gradually loosened as the majority of his supporters (including the PKI, which constituted a major part of his power base) were eliminated, discredited, or frightened into submission. When Sukarno finally relinquished the presidency under extreme pressure in 1967, the absolute power of the New Order regime, which had in essence already been running the country for two years, was swiftly and smoothly officialized under the leadership of Suharto. While sources quote differing numbers of victims of the "emergency" actions that brought the New Order to power, they all suggest the total killed to be between 500,000 and 2 million at the very least.[4]

During the chaotic, transitional period during which the killings occurred, Suharto and the military gained control over the populace by mapping and dividing the country along a stark, categorical line: nationalist/patriot versus communist/traitor. Via the mass media and a coalition of conservative Islamic leaders, those thought to be associated with the PKI, which was saddled with the blame for the attempted coup and the resulting deaths of the generals, were claimed by the military to be both morally depraved and atheist. As such, they were portrayed as a serious threat to the continuing practice of established religious and cultural norms and to public safety in general. "Kill or be killed," said the military: eradicate the "murderous" PKI before it rose up and destroyed the nation.

In this context, with Suharto and the Army occupying the position of nationalist, anyone perceived as a potential threat to their power was quickly identified as communist and treated as part of an enemy force. While the military led and carried out the majority of killings and arrests of suspected PKI members, civilian collaborators and paramilitaries were also an important factor in the staging of violence on such a massive scale. Thus, with the urgency of the struggle between "good" and "evil" thoroughly established, and with much of the citizenry involved—albeit mainly through coercion—in its bloody actualization, the groundwork for Suharto's rise was laid: the majority of the populace was now either complicit, utterly terrorized, or, more likely, both. The military's claims that the killing and imprisonment of those ostensibly opposed to its authority was socially and politically "justified" thus went unchallenged, despite the lack of any sort of due process.

The same strategy was later applied by the New Order government regarding its long-term claims to power and legitimacy of rule. Following from this, Suharto's initial techniques of suppression and control were continued—and exponentially expanded. Former political prisoners and their families, bearing the official label of "unclean," were subject to pervasive, highly detailed forms of scrutiny and persecution throughout the thirty-year dictatorship. In the climate of suspicion and fear bred by the Suharto regime, accusations of leftist subversion (and the severe punishment that would follow) served to irredeemably taint the reputations of those targeted in the eyes of authorities, neighbors, and frequently even relatives. Virtually overnight, accused dissidents became permanent second-class citizens and were denied numerous rights, including access to education, proper identity cards, or eligibility for most forms of desirable employment.[5] The government also forbade "leftists" to publicly perform or privately practice many forms of traditional culture, including dance and other performing arts, and prohibited them from expressing their thoughts or developing their own narratives regarding the events of recent history.[6]

State Narration of Female Alliances: Sexualized "Communist" Bodies

Many of those affected by the New Order's massive societal recategorization were artists, a large percentage of whom were female. Of the women arrested, imprisoned, or eliminated by the New Order, a significant number were also targeted because of their involvement in an artists' guild known as Lekra (the People's Cultural Institution), as well as the protofeminist women's organization Gerwani, both of which were associated with the progressive left of the 1950s and '60s.[7] (Despite their generally socialist leanings, however, the membership of these groups was connected with many different parties and thus was *not* necessarily communist or affiliated with the PKI).[8] In the context of Indonesia's transition to authoritarian rule under Suharto, the class-based social justice advocated by Lekra, and particularly the gender politics promoted by Gerwani, were seen as threatening to the idealized national identity promoted by the emerging New Order regime.

After terrorizing and eliminating the guilds' members (along with accused members of the PKI), the state later claimed that these groups, which promoted working-class and women's rights, were directly and/or indirectly supporting communist ideas and practices through the ideology of "equality" that they advertised. In most cases, however, the goals of Lekra, Gerwani, and other related organizations had been to raise awareness of basic human needs, such as reducing work hours for pregnant women, demanding bathroom facilities in factories, or dancing and singing songs that questioned policies regarding gender equality or articulated specific notions of longing and difference. Such songs often used "traditional" arts idioms to communicate these ideas, where the use of the idioms enabled a semi-veiled critique of the status quo, frequently targeting and satirizing certain established social practices such as polygamy and women's limited rights to education. The commitment of many Lekra and Gerwani members to populist, "folk"-based artistic practices, and the fact that under Sukarno they were often hired to perform at political rallies and events—including those of the PKI—were also viewed as threatening to both the emerging Suharto state and to the deep-rooted presence of Islamic patriarchal rule on the local level.[9]

In the context of 1965, the power of women dancers and singers in particular to draw large, attentive crowds at various assemblies and gatherings seemed not to be lost on either the emerging state or the long-standing patriarchal establishment. After the rise of the New Order, the artistic practices of accused subversives, especially those of women associated with Lekra and Gerwani, were banned by the state (although many were later reintroduced after having been "cleansed"), while performers were forced to disavow the practices under the threat of imprisonment and death. Afterward, there was no effort to compensate artists for lost livelihoods or to reexamine the violence done to them. Because the killing, imprisonment, and censure of progressive female practitioners in particular essentially functioned to shore up the position of existing village leadership, in most cases the rural patriarchal establishment was actively complicit with the military and emerging state in the carrying out of these acts.[10]

In my analysis, the claiming of certain artistic practices by the state, and the later replacement of their vanished or banned practitioners with state representatives, constitute the conditions of possibility for Indonesia's national culture after 1965, as well as its oft-touted, yet equally calculated and exclusive, "cultural diversity." (Here, a small sampling of regional forms are likewise claimed "polished" and then performed by state-aligned bodies as a projection of the state's democratic self-image.) In this book I document the process of the establishment of these art forms as national cultural traditions by the New Order. Composing a crucial element of Indonesia's reformulated national identity as instituted under Suharto, the practices were vigorously promoted by the state in both the domestic and international arenas. At home, they were disseminated via the national educational curriculum and regional and national festivals. Abroad, Indonesia's renegotiation of its position on the stage of international politics involved the strategic foregrounding of its cultural heritage—in most cases involving dancing women as vehicles of expression.

Thus, the nation, having been "quietly"[11] reformulated during Suharto's rise and under his subsequent iron-fisted rule, began ingratiating and enmeshing itself anew within the complex web of alliances based on the Cold War and the West's global project of multiculturalism. In many instances I view the presence of such politics of "diversity" as a tragedy and forced forgetting, a forgetting that serves, among other things, to politically and economically stabilize a government that would otherwise be precariously balanced upon the memories, stories, songs, dances, and bones of millions of Indonesians. Using this frame of time and place, then, I examine the ways in which culture becomes engendered as a tool to mediate the needs of the nation-state and foreign institutional agendas in their cultural projects. My concerns are how culture is evaluated and commodified through the global process of aesthetic exchange and Third World economic development, and further, how this commodification transpires within the practice of multiculturalism in Indonesia and abroad. How does women's citizenship, in relation to state patriarchy, become both mobile and "flexible" in the context of serving global capital? And, finally, in what ways might women be able to intervene in the cultural construction of Indonesia in order to mediate their own representation as figures with a broad, complex, and fraught political and cultural history?

When Memory Becomes Speech:
A Fleeting Moment of Inclusion and *Reformasi*

After nearly half a century, the effects of the terrible rise of Suharto and the reign of the New Order are perhaps more palpable than ever, particularly as survivors begin to reconsolidate, recount, and reconstruct their memories in ever more open attempts to narrate their experiences. In 2005, after forty years, the first-ever public memorialization of the events of 1965, held by those who were targeted and victimized by the state and their supporters, took place in Jakarta.[12] The weeklong affair was composed of talks, panel discussions, and various performances and film screenings by and about the survivors of the New Order's campaigns of terror. The events attracted many people, including academics from the Jakarta Institute of the Arts, University of Indonesia, members of youth organizations, nongovernmental organizations (NGOs) from the capital city and Yogyakarta *(Syarikat),* and dozens of former political prisoners. Many of these *"ekstapol,"*[13] as those previously held by order of the state are officially referred to, were attending the event in affiliation with the group Yayasan Penelitian Korban Pembunuhan 1965–1966 (Indonesian Institute for the Study of the 1965–1966 Massacres, founded in Jakarta on April 17, 1999, less than a year after the fall of Suharto). At the time, I was following the cases of some of the *ekstapol* with great interest, as many of them had been persistently approaching the courts to petition for justice, under the guise of a semi-formalized movement they called, in English, "Clash Action." A week prior to the memorial event, the former political prisoners also made the unprecedented move of marching in front of the Istana Negara (the presidential palace in Jakarta).

The gathering of survivors in the context of the memorial, a reunion of sorts, formed a strong visible presence throughout the week, and particularly during the many performances at the Jakarta Goethe Institute on the night of September 30, the date used each year by the state to commemorate Suharto's "heroism" in eradicating the Communist Party. Among the many speakers was the former president Abdurrahman Wahid (leader of Nahdatul Ulama, Indonesia's largest Islamic association); "Gus Dur," as he was affectionately known, was elected shortly after the fall of Suharto in 1998. As president, he became the first Indonesian public figure to acknowledge that the events of 1965 were an abuse of human rights, and he took the unprecedented step of officially asking forgiveness from the family members of the New Order's victims. To the disappointment of many, however, he was unable to change the constitution Ketetapan Majelis Permusyawaratan Rakyat Sementara XXV 1966 (TAP MPRS) in regard to this matter, and, due to his stance on 1965 and a variety of other factors, lost the support of Parliament soon after his election and was forced to resign from the presidency. However, like many others, I continue to view the late Gus Dur and the members of groups like Clash Action both as important allies and as irreplaceable sources of history, memory, and experience.

In many ways, this book constitutes my own attempt to collaborate and to further the important work of such figures by investigating and interrogating the continual erasure of the stories of those who were killed or disappeared or survived years of cruel imprisonment in the many island gulags and state prisons throughout the archipelago, and the covering up of the physical traces left by their bodies and the histories of violence perpetrated upon them. I view such actions as bringing about, for those "vanished"—or more specifically for their surviving relatives and colleagues considered tainted by association—what Edward Said calls "paradoxical citizenship." As John Ochoa explains, the term refers to a position, like Said's own, in which the possibility of "belonging" to an actual homeland has been utterly destroyed by historical circumstance. Yet despite the profound shock of disconnection and loss, which is often linked to madness, some, like Said, have managed to put their unrootedness to use. As a critic, he was often inspired by the experiences of other prolific thinkers who lived in various modes of exile: "The more one is able to leave one's own cultural home more easily is one able to judge it."[14] Like the *ekstapol* calling for justice from a state that has disclaimed their very existence as true citizens, in my own position as a genealogically subversive dancer whose critical work rests on the fragility of access to both outside thought and inside information, I find a sense of comfort, as well as hope, in Ochoa's reading of Said: "The critic of true vision, one who avoids complicity with hegemonic powers . . . must be buoyed by a constant otherness within his own critique." Yet ultimately, as he points out, "this perpetual displacement required for 'true vision,' this permanent 'elsewhereness' is obviously paradoxical—paradoxical citizenship."[15]

Perhaps, however, what might be thought of as the obverse of such a circumstance in Indonesia could be called "paradoxical statehood," since a nation founded on mass exclusion and murder will in all likelihood give birth to millions of "inspired" critics, whose long periods of silence may signify—rather than national stability—a collective waiting for a moment of speaking that will, in the end, arrive. Driven, then, by the gradual narrowing of the gap that precedes me, I seek to open a new, dialectical space within collective memory: to illustrate the ways in which the cultural practices of a vast number of Indonesia's burgeoning proletariat were claimed by the state, without reparations or reexamination of the violence done to them, and how their bodies were replaced by other bodies, bodies that must continually pledge and show their allegiance to nation and government.

Following Caren Kaplan, I view the New Order state's extraction and reclamation of performing arts as a pointed deterritorialization of tradition—an attempt to remove cultural practice from "the conditions of resistance and opposition that most people in the world have no choice but to struggle for."[16] As such the state's actions are always already a "reterritorialization, an increase of territory, an imperialization"[17] in which the actor "paradoxically" erases the marks of its own politically motivated maneuvering.

In the hands of New Order ideology, then, grasping the reins of control that still bore the marks of the Dutch conquerors' grip, Indonesian cultural practice appeared to float effortlessly among its local, national, and global levels of production and display. The creation of meaning and context within these spatial and cultural locations thus functioned to provide an idealized social and political value. As the massacres cut the connection between certain dances and the bodies that practiced them, the continuation of dance was structured through the agency of the centralized state. Thus, while thousands of practitioners lay buried in mass graves or were socially and economically incapacitated, the aesthetics of Indonesian dance continued to flourish and travel in apparent transcendence of the borders of experience and nationality.

The Relocation and Circulation of New Order Narrative: Not Simply a "Cultural Transmission"

Dance tradition, in the construction of national identity, is based on an imaginary past,[18] the concept of its preserved value, and the acknowledgment of the brilliant bodies of the "virtuous" citizens who

Performance of *Jaran Goyang* by Indonesian state troupe in Fukuoka, Japan, 2000. Dancer: Erlina Pantja Sulistjaningtyas. Copyright: Erlina Pantja Sulistjaningtyas.

master the technique and who transmit and reproduce it through the limited, legitimized channels of ethnic groups, nation, and government. As such it often represents hegemonic alliances (that is, established dominant bodies) within nation-states.[19] This deterritorialization of dance tradition creates its image as a practice that appears to be genealogically or socially transmitted through embodied performance and the continuation of embedded values and meaning.

In the context of Indonesia, while tradition promoted by the state is utilized as a tool to showcase the unification of differences within the extremely diverse and culturally, linguistically, and geographically fragmented populace, the process itself is not based on the understanding of complexity in the conceptualization of citizenship and belonging. It forces groups to form cultural alliances that are often categorized based on geographical state alone; for example, Java versus Bali or Sumatra versus Papua. In general those islands farthest from Java, both ethnically and geographically, have the lowest levels of participatory access in national culture. Here, borrowing Smadar Lavie's term, we might say that the bodily, or *somatic,* experience[20] of inclusion (within centralized traditional discourse) determines the cultural value for practitioners. In response, I affirm the complexity of cultural production in the context of dance and the dancing body, particularly when they are categorized as traditional in reference to certain ethnic groups.[21] My own experience with traditional practices has led me to consider the theoretical questions surrounding the discourse of cultural preservation and the political economy of tradition as well as the possibilities—and great potential challenges—of creating a resistant project.

To analyze the complex relationship between preserved dance traditions and the global role of institutionalizing practice, then, I begin by finding a pattern through which the canonization of the ideology of cultural origin and its discourse on "native culture" is implemented. (The location of implementation of such discourse, of course, is usually separate from that of its founding, since it is usually attributed to former colonizers, or foreign organizations based in the First World.)[22] In this context, I focus on Indonesia without escaping the historiography of colonialism and the process of modern state formation, which reconfigures the nation's identity as postcolonial.[23] I study the ways in which the mechanisms of continuity and the transformation of tradition are accomplished as well as reflected by the practitioners of culture and performing arts (as in Michel Foucault's rights of citizenship).[24] I also recognize practitioners' complex relationships with their own nation-states, where such individual efforts are possible and expected yet bound within the condition of obeying the parameters of order, which, as Achille Mbembe argues, "although precarious, are always in the making, in an ongoing process of fragile actualization."[25]

My analysis also examines the way marginal groups of women have survived and maintained their "forbidden" artistic practices in the face of continual stigmatization and oppression, a phenomenon that provides me with a moment to rethink the concept of access and public acknowledgment as absolute indicators of value in traditional practice. Yet the outward domination of state-defined access continues to this day, with the government discourse about 1965 and its aftermath still firmly embedded within the educational, social, and political systems. After the fall of Suharto in 1998, there was some degree of change in human rights abuse cases, and many remaining political prisoners were released, while those in exile were permitted to reenter the country. Yet the shadow of the New Order power structure, with its co-optation and monitoring of citizens on many different levels, looms large, and the justice process, plagued by the intervention of myriad powerful interests with direct ties to Suharto's regime, has been stilted and far from comprehensive. For example, in 2006, despite seeming to loosen its grip in other areas, the government began cracking down on publishers of new textbooks that diverged, only very slightly, from the New Order-era state narrative on 1965. The result, which brought the continuing historical relevance of 1965 into sharp focus, was the nationwide banning and public burning of the books in question in 2007.

Thus, despite the fall of Suharto and the implementation of a more open and "democratic" system of governance in Indonesia, the familiar narratives in which victims of state violence and their families are transformed into traitors and pariahs continue to circulate. This official account, as before, is told through history books, national monuments and museums, and public school teachers, who continue to function as civil servants under the direct purview of the state. Government narratives are also available through a variety of other media, in particular the continuing existence of films that were once required annual viewing for all schoolchildren; while no longer obligatory, there are, as of yet, no widely publicized accounts of the historical inaccuracies or explicit ideological motivations of such movies.[26]

In the context of the present *Reformasi* era (following 1998, when Suharto stepped down), this complicated history intersects with ongoing struggles for economic and political rights and extends to control over the civic sphere through the network of artists who are also civil servants, and therefore are active in academic life and the development of Indonesian scholarship. Buyung Nasution, a human rights activist and lawmaker, has said that Suharto's worst crime is to have made Indonesians afraid to think and express themselves.[27] In 1998,

Human Rights Watch similarly traced many of the most insidious problems created by the New Order to its multileveled infiltration of the national education system:

> As Soeharto consolidated his power . . . he eventually turned his attention on the universities, which were emerging as a leading source of opposition to the authoritarian policies of the new government and the increasing political prominence of the military. In response to student protest movements in the 1970s, the government twice cracked down hard on the academic community. Although the effects were most pronounced in the social sciences and the humanities, the government's repressive response to the protests had devastating consequences for academic freedom and for freedom of expression in society more generally.[28]

Thus the state of the national education system, still bearing the effects of frequent government infiltration and intimidation, perpetuates an air of fear and stigmatization around efforts to rehistoricize the events of 1965 and the New Order era.

The national cultural identity produced in post-1965 Indonesia enabled the state's high level of societal control precisely because of its rapid reconfiguration and submergence within the established reality of daily life, working in concert with the "voluntary" participation of Indonesian citizens and the international support and demand for nationalized art forms on the global stage. Drawing on the New Order state as a primary example, in my analysis of the production of cultural identity, I follow Moriana Gomez and Mercedes Duran-Cogan, who suggest that cultural values are promulgated by local negotiation and circumscribed by a process of inclusion and exclusion. From this perspective, identity formation is a "complex object of knowledge that can only be examined in its mediation, that is at the crossroads where historical contexts, socio political processes, and artistic or non-artistic, verbal or non verbal, representation interact."[29]

Historically, specific information regarding the mass killings of 1965 was muted both nationally and internationally, while the nation focused on its internal "development project," deciding how best to present Indonesia to the international political, economic, and cultural policymakers. In the postindependence environment, the state perhaps realized that there was still a significant global demand for exoticism, and it was there that the nation could find its niche. Exoticism, with its emphasis on spirituality and religiosity, indirectly nurtures the colonial fantasy of the West toward Indonesia (and much of the rest of the East and Africa) and successfully legitimizes the new cultural representations that Indonesia's New Order regime reconstructed; it simultaneously erases the violence perpetrated against historical Indonesian bodies, and in particular Indonesian women's bodies. As Gayatri Spivak has argued this point, "between patriarchy and imperialism, subject-constitution and object-formation, the figure of the woman disappears, not into pristine nothingness, but into a violent shuttling that displaces figuration of the 'third world women' caught between tradition and modernization, culturalism and development."[30] Drawing on Spivak to analyze women's positions in Indonesia, I argue that this new space in cultural production and its relationship to global space needs to be reexamined. Until now, it has for the most part been co-opted by the continuation of the New Order's amnesia project, as cultural production once practiced by unwanted groups was reclaimed by the state as "embedded in society," yet was performed solely by new, historically "clean" bodies aligned with state political doctrine. This cloned, enclosed system, consisting of pre–New Order practice performed and disseminated by "replicas" of the bodies of vanished artists, then became the source of the nation-state's cultural identity.

From the vantage point provided by this system, cultural practices in Indonesia appear to be a pure, authentic, or undiluted traditional heritage. However, in their integral, interdependent, and temporally based relationship to statehood, such art forms might be viewed in terms of Benedict Anderson's discussion of nationalism as a particular kind of "cultural artifact." For Anderson, nationalism is a "modular" concept formed by a complex permutation of historical forces and "capable of being transplanted, with varying degrees of self consciousness, to a great variety of social terrains . . . [and] political and ideological constellations."[31] In my analysis, the reproduction of dance practice within a rather modular—and well-used—sense of tradition serves to obscure not only the historical violence on which the nation was founded, but the intricate process of variation and

change that leads to the long-standing establishment of certain practices as well as their categorization as "traditional" or "heritage."

Because of my own historical journey, experiences, and obser-
vations, I am also aware that the space of national cultural (re)pro-
duction can provide great mobility and access to its official—and at
times its unofficial—practitioners. This is especially true for those
artists who seem to "naturally" embody the re-narrativization of
postcolonial local or national identity and the historiography of
the practice in relation to the demands of the contemporary global
stage or cultural market. (Here I understand the postcolonial on
the global stage as an effort to perform traditional dance as an ideal
Other in the midst of the modern/postmodern/avant garde community.) Yet I invite such artists to rethink and examine their own
histories and the specific lineages of their practice more closely.[32]
Invoking Benedict Anderson's notion of nations as historical expressions of "cultural roots" that are assumed to be both collective and
"timeless,"[33] I hope to provoke a debate among practitioners as to
whether they bear a certain responsibility to "act out" their own
embodied historicity. Here I urge a consideration of the potential of
highly developed techniques for corporeal communication to perform the knowledge and memories necessarily embedded in dancers' bodies and inside the practices that they have, in fact, despite
the many interventions of the state and others, *inherited* from those
who came before them.

It is my view that mobility, particularly for those who enact art
forms such as dance, can become a powerful form of resistance[34] to
dominant and dominating cultural and political narratives. In constructing networks through the conception of our movements as a
"transnational feminist practice"—based on the need to address the
responses of a number of non-Western states to local and national histories in terms of culture and gender-based display—we may begin
to form alliances that provide a more critical space within which to
examine the hegemony of local patriarchal rule and its connections
to international structures of power. In other words, this new networking of international artists can provide a space for Indonesian
feminist practices to look for transitions in a location where the state's
power is less clear and absolute, as the presence of a militaristic style

of maintaining order continues to impose itself in subtle, and again increasingly not so subtle, ways at home. These alliances should serve to complicate understandings of movement as a distinctly somatic experience, as it is shown to be formed, and informed, dispersedly through varied networks of social strata that may chance to meet when artists cross borders.[35]

Locating Diaspora: The (Re)Marketing of National Culture for the Global Stage

In formulating the possibility of resistant alliances across and outside of national boundaries, I am aware of the potential risk of association with pro-globalization movements calling for the complete dissolution of borders as a form of "dissent." In the mere existence of cultural practice in the global or international arena, dance performances at some level become reducible to a mass of discrete traditional art forms that locate themselves as binary Other in the midst of Western standard techniques. This identification with (non)location is implicated in the new discourse of "worlding" dance, which effectively divorces forms from the realities of social, political, and historical contexts.[36] Worlded performances can thus be interpreted as existing in a globalized multicultural space, as part of a gesture toward diversity or an attempt to recognize the "Other" from the centrist viewpoint of European- and American-based productions. As Ananya Chatterjea argues, "There are also those genres or kinds of work that, produced in 'minority' communities in keeping with an official mandate, get signed on by mainstream Western culture as acceptable markers of 'ethnic'/'non-Western' cultures."[37] Many works performed on the global stage (in which I include the diasporic practices of migrants, among others) are provided for, and economically initiated by, European and American resources in order to fulfill the demands of what I call "the global diversity project." If, within this global stage, there is an Asian regional level, it is mostly provided for and initiated by the more economically established countries and city-states such as Japan, Singapore, Hong Kong, and, owing to its recent leadership in modern and postmodern dance and scholarship in Asia, Taiwan. Thus, we find that this intercultural region of arts production is also

strongly dependent on dominant global economic and political posi-
tionings and alliances.

If we look at a nation such as Indonesia, we will, of course, find
many spaces providing cross-cultural or inter-/intracultural performance that are more concerned with local or regional values. However, because of the deeply rooted, unspoken, and as yet unresolved
problems such as the history of mass murder, ongoing stigmatization
and violence to the body, and complex webs of artistic and political exclusion and inclusion, an implicit question arises: Is the fragmented, factionalized, and co-opted "intracultural" performance in
Indonesia—as Rustom Bharucha suggests in the case of intercultural
arts Asia in general—doomed to failure, and, if so, is it still conceiv-
able that "the very vulnerabilities, limitations and failures of our . . .
endeavours can ignite new possibilities of change?"[38]

If the basic challenge to most Indonesian citizens is to deal with
the poverty and injustice that still dominates daily life, how can we
possibly shape resistant alliances among ourselves without addressing
the myriad, unresolved suspicions and fears at the local level? This
question opens a space for us to examine the "cultural sustainability concept" coined by United Nations Educational, Scientific and
Cultural Organization (UNESCO)—in terms of both "tangible" and
"intangible" aspects of cultural practice—as well as to question the
Indonesian state's copyright system, which views cultural practices as
material and as state-held intellectual property. "Indigenous dance" or
music under this rubric is decontextualized, deterritorialized from its
political history, and reterritorialized as state apparatus. Who, under
this system, is capable of movement? Who can travel to national or
international stages with the practice in their bodies, and where does
it "come from"? Can we imagine a practitioner who embodies the
dance in such a way as to stage an alternate reterritorialization in the
name of history? Where might such an act take place?

My examination, then, does not lead to a conclusion or a justification for rejecting this global stage—be it inter- or intracultural, or
whatever term we might feel comfortable using—but rather seeks to
question the ways in which we may reexamine and reexplore this space
while simultaneously testing the limits of such an exploration. Thus, as
the international and the global are interconnected through the local,

my question is, Will the global stage be able to provide for the local needs that still exist—for dancers, artists, and other citizens alike—on a daily basis, and at the most basic level of human rights? How does the interconnection of policy among states, especially within the sphere of foreign affairs and economic development, affect those who try to build their own artistic "free trade zone," to which the border-crossing "flexibility"[39] of their citizenship and creative skills—valued by governments as nationalist labor—may provide access?

As a dancer and academic active in international circles of cultural exchange, will belonging to this new space enable me to access my own zone of freedom, or is it a clear co-optation that will become a point of departure for an eventual failure of my postcolonial critique in favor of my access to base mobility? Is it possible to dance on the mass grave while at the same time illuminating the global stage's (in)capacity to challenge the unspoken injustices to the body, a history that easily disappears in the glamour of international travel and performance?

History, of course, must itself be illuminated in relation to the confluence of global forces, alliances, and political trends as they intersect with and influence the national and the local in particular ways. During his tenure as Indonesia's first president, from 1945 until 1967, Sukarno began exploring the possibility of a new relationship with China based on trade and economic cooperation and was greatly interested in establishing other common interests and fostering collaboration and exchange. This potential alliance caused great concern within the staunchly anti-communist U.S. government, especially since Indonesia's Communist Party had, by the early 1960s, become the third largest in the world. According to Baskara Wardaya, this was due in part to the problematics of Indonesia's "young" political system during the 1950s—"In fact it seemed there was a possibility that the masses would not be fully included in the nation building process. If this was true, perhaps it is not surprising that the PKI . . . in a short time developed [a large] following"[40]— and a very strong position within the nation's multiparty "guided democracy." In 1958, concerned about both the growing influence of the Communist Party and the strong general political and economic resistance to the West fostered by Sukarno, the United States initiated a plan of indirect intervention in Indonesia in the form of logistical and financial support for the establishment of a military junta under Suharto.[41]

As discussed previously, the resulting massacres brought about a new form of state representation in which a highly uniform conception of national culture was brought to the fore. As a constructed cultural disposition that was presented both domestically and internationally, New Order national identity essentially functioned to locate Indonesian citizens and the leaders and officers of foreign nations quite similarly with regard to local history: both were ultimately expected to occupy something of an "outside" point of view, from which the complex webs of violence and domination—as well as various forms of resistance—that had given shape to contemporary, local artistic practice were difficult, or impossible, to discern. Strategizing the continuing reputation of Indonesia as peaceful, yet highly colorful and exotic, the central government also strove to produce images of great ethnic and cultural diversity that simultaneously promoted a homogenous, unified representation of Indonesia as a single nation. Because of its highly effective controls on the spread of information, even during and shortly after the massacres, the New Order was able to move quickly to establish a far-reaching influence over cultural practices. This was accomplished with the support of practitioners—particularly the countless young inductees into the national arts and education systems in the early years of the Suharto era—who themselves in many instances may not have been aware of the effects of their cooperation.

As displayed in both domestic and global contexts, state-sponsored depictions of national culture have typically emphasized "high" court culture and Hindu epic–based performance to the exclusion of various other forms and the groups that perform them, as defined, among other things, by ethnicity, class, location, and experience. This process as it occurs in Indonesia profoundly dismisses internal political and social struggles. For example, the presentation of cultural forms from Papua—a large region of Indonesia that has frequently voted to secede—is extremely rare in official, nationally publicized events or at international diplomatic meetings. In this case the visibility of cultural, aesthetic, and political difference within the generalized global Otherness projected by the state is minimized in contexts in which they might draw particular attention to the discontinuities and gaps in the discourse of national unity and harmony among local ethnic groups.

Yet despite its suppression of unruly difference, the state's project of "Indonesianization," or cultural homogenization, must still be seen as operating within the framework of exoticism. This national self-exoticism occurs, for example, through the prominence of the female body, specifically in the placement of the female performer as the object of the spectatorial gaze in most state-sanctioned performances. In the most frequently displayed forms—those based in Balinese Hindu ritual practice or Javanese dance dramas taken from the *Mahabarata* and *Ramayana* epics—the female dancer is most often portrayed as a goddess, princess, or other fetishistic icon of patriarchal desire. Such typified exoticism, as Savigliano suggests, is of course the product of a cultural "industry," one which survives by circulating "emotional capital" and thereby "stirring the blood of up-until-then oblivious bodies, driving them into complicitous acknowledgments of each other."[42]

Pembinaan: The Strategic Centralization of Culture through the Concept of Value

A major element of Indonesia's self-marketing as a nation with a rich traditional culture is its claim to the "unification" of more than 17,000 islands and thousands of ethnic groups, languages, and ecologies into a singular, pluralistic national cultural identity. The use of women performers as signifiers of a peaceful diversity that is simultaneously enticingly exotic has become central to Indonesia's marketization of culture and representation of nationhood. Because its strategy involves a tightly intertwined, two-pronged commodification and exportation of culture, in the local context, the homogenization of nationalized culture has had a profound effect on regional expression, having for the most part become a dominant concern even at the village level. The dissemination of this effect is orchestrated by the national cultural policy known as *pembinaan*.

In definition, *pembinaan* is translated as "to make better," coming from the root word *bina,* which means "construct" in the sense of improving or uplifting something. The concept of *pembinaan* thus contains an intrinsic value judgment, often a blatantly discriminatory one, upon the existing form that must be *dibina,* or trained and further developed, labeling it as inherently lacking or less. In effect, the artists required to go through the process of *pembinaan* are mostly from rural village contexts (and mostly practice "folk dance"); those who institute and perform *pembinaan* are state-employed civil servants or government officers. After local groups or artists are judged to have become sufficiently *dibina*—in alignment with official cultural standards—if they are "lucky," they may gain access to state support, which usually means obtaining permits to practice and perform in contexts or venues outside of the village setting. They may receive financial incentives as well, known as *uang pembinaan,* a small amount of money that is normally put toward raising production values, often by designing and purchasing new costumes or orienting performances toward more lucrative urban or tourist audiences.

The process of *pembinaan* brings small, but not insignificant, changes to dance forms. In addition to the altering of costumes and/ or makeup, movements may be directed to appear more synchronized and controlled (standardized), as improvisation or spontaneous interpretations are reduced or eliminated. Therefore, while such local forms are not likely to play a major role in the large-scale formation of national identity—they are not apt to be included in widespread educational curricula or exported performance programs—even as a marginal cultural product, they have entered the system of state control and valuation in cooperation with local capitalism. Thus, the local government's branch of the Ministry of Culture, be it in the *desa* (village), *kecamatan* (district), or *kabupaten* (regional or provincial level), implements the nationalization of local cultural practices according to centralized policy. Yet as we will see, the village context, as a long-standing site for the production of value in folk arts, has at times provided continuing testimony to the powerful and empowering effects of such practice when wielded by nonaligned artists whom central authorities would otherwise cast out.

At both village and national levels, however, the commodification of dance is also connected to the local effects of international efforts to promote and implement "development" and "progress," both terms that refer to the discourse of industry and the distribution of labor but also affect cultural practices. After the period of mass killings in 1965–66, the U.S. involvement in Indonesia shifted from political and military affairs to the arenas of economics and culture. George Aditjondro, an Indonesian scholar, explains that the massacres, in ridding Indonesia of its left-leaning, anti-Western identity, directly built the basis for subsequent foreign investment as well as for Suharto's immense personal accumulation of wealth within the new, more "open" economic environment.[43] In this context, the approach to shaping cultural policy has drawn directly from economics-based concepts like sustainability, so that the ideals of cultural preservation are largely determined by the capital-driven impulses of development and productivity.

Examples of this kind of cultural policy are evident in the local funding decisions made by the United States and international associations such as UNESCO, underlining the connections between the global approach to diversity and cultural and local violence. Although UNESCO is an international body, its work focuses primarily on Third World countries, or countries that are looked on as poor and underdeveloped, in which culture is often considered to be under threat from rapid change (which is normally associated with the encroachment of modernity and globalized media rather than the violence perpetrated on practitioners by the state). In chapters 3 and 4 of this book, I refer to the involvement of UNESCO in Indonesia— and comparatively to its work in Cambodia—in order to better understand the entanglements of states' agendas and the management of cultural heritage in relation to histories of violence. Specifically targeting these kinds of regions, UNESCO operates within universalized standards of progress and development, according to which these countries are considered behind in their level of industrialization and in many cases in their political transparency or so-called democratization. The prevalent conception of UNESCO's leadership of certain countries is that these nations are in need of economic and often political help, but also that they have something to share or contribute to the broader international community in terms of their apparent surplus of culture. Therefore, the preservation and sustainability of certain customs and artistic practices becomes an important project for international funding bodies like UNESCO. As a result, local cultural forms are contextualized not entirely on their own terms but within the global discourse of uneven economic development.

The rhetoric of preservation also significantly affects the continuing study and practice of cultural forms. Key cultural policies in both Cambodia and Indonesia align with UNESCO's policy of cultural preservation known as "intangible cultural heritage."[44] Intangible cultural heritage is said to define something of value in a certain society that is not physical, something that is to be preserved and protected (*physical* here means material, and related to intellectual property, which is the other "half" of cultural practice that is claimed by the state; thus, each organization takes its share and leaves practitioners with few rights). This policy of course is subject to the decisions of UNESCO as to which specific cultural practices are granted the opportunity to be locally and globally preserved, both financially through international funding and via worldwide legal and copyright arrangements. Here I argue that this policy distributes benefits only to highly select groups of people—most often those already chosen for the value they provide the state—and discourages attempts by practitioners themselves to reinterpret their own culture, history, or artistic practices, leading to a stagnation in time and place that may indeed function as a support system for repressive government policies promoting stability through the silencing of dissent.

International cultural philanthropy such as that practiced and promoted by UNESCO is based on the notion that these cultures, and the national or political entities attached to them, are not only in some sense threatened by globalization but are also endangered by politically volatile situations (particularly those in which the aggressors are *not* aligned with Western power), lack of economic resources, and/or fragile security. This view is used to justify particular kinds of investment and cultural preservation in the so-called Third World, where modernization and economic development are carefully monitored in terms of their perceived potential to overwhelm or destroy the particular cultural heritages that the West and other powerful Eastern nations have chosen as representatives of global multiculturalism. Thus, rather than having a mandate for the preservation of cultural life on a per-culture basis or interest in living artistic practices, international cultural policy emphasizes the preservation of traditional art forms as authentic, involving the active prevention of such forms going through a process of change or encountering any kind of new interpretation, approach, or expansion. Such activities are also limited by their cost, which local funding is often not sufficient to cover; in Indonesia after the rise of the New Order, the co-optation of ritual practice by the state in connection with sources of subsidy and development from outside agencies has produced and enabled much of the politically motivated reinvention of national culture as "tradition." The work produced under this system then becomes part of the list of activities supported by philanthropic institutions in order to serve diversity, albeit most often in the context of a Western or global audience nostalgically traveling back in time, "exploring the orient."

However, while external funding sources frequently intervene in national arts production, such sources are, of course, only one part of the complex internal processes that allow local performances and cultural practices to be exported to the United States and elsewhere. National deployment of cultural diplomacy remains the most significant factor, as it places Indonesian performing arts, and dance in particular, in a prominent position within state-to-state interaction between Indonesia and other nations: in addition to current trade and foreign aid agreements with the U.S. government and other governments, Indonesia has, since independence, produced and sent so-called cultural missions on international diplomatic tours, with one or two performances usually held in each nation along the way. Longer-term workshops, residencies, or collaborations, however, which bring Indonesians into closer contact with Western artists, students, and audiences, are for the most part initiated by the United States or other economically powerful nations that have the philanthropic resources to invite and accommodate performers; those considered for such programs are usually artists who are already established within the national or global economy of culture as masters of their craft. At the same time, for example, the granting of U.S. funds to support artistic exchange is always mediated by U.S. foreign policy and, in turn, the variable and often unpredictable strictures of immigration policy. Within these circles of artistic exchange, female performing artists participate at many levels in the cultural construction of the Indonesian nation-state through performance, choreography, and bodily practice. While the process necessarily involves cooperation and thus co-optation by state power, artists nonetheless retain a certain potential to intervene. Possessing a sense of artistic ownership (which is, however, by no means a copyright or legal ownership) as lead practitioners of the Indonesian traditional forms most highly valued within the cultural construction process, women lay claim to and signify a certain strain of authority in the development of national representation, both domestically and in relation to the global market. In addition, since dance training has become part of the national education curriculum, female artists play an important role in the construction of a "national culture" in their position as educators. The practice of performing arts, therefore, provides mobility for women by enabling them to engage in the state education system. Yet at the same time, the women necessarily become functionaries of the system.

The potential for agency, then, is at best dialectical—at worst, simply paradoxical—and heavily dependent on context and individual achievements and access. In the Indonesian academic context, certain female performing artists are afforded opportunities to experiment with contemporary approaches to traditional dance and to explore current themes, as long as the themes avoid touching upon government policies connected with particular political events. This experimentation is also often facilitated by funds from foreign institutions, and to a small degree by the Indonesian Ministry of Culture and Tourism, the Ministry of Education, and the Ministry of Foreign Affairs. Through this process, women not only participate but also produce and choreograph new works, as part of the construction of national culture in Indonesia, opening at least the possibility for the expression of certain elements of historical experience within national arts projects, albeit within a system that still functions with the explicit goal of enriching the state and its national culture.

Although women face major obstacles in developing and presenting new forms of expression and in challenging entrenched policies and social norms, in certain instances they have begun to directly address restrictions placed on them through committed joint efforts forged across the country. Even though funding for contemporary projects may come from institutions with their own agendas, the artists themselves are not necessarily directly limited by categories like "Third World," "developing country," or other markers imposed by sources of foreign funding. Through their participation in cultural construction, then, female performing artists are able to subtly redefine the relationship between women and the state-center. While women are still foregrounded as objects of the male gaze, they also negotiate and adjust their positions in state patriarchy, imbuing the role of "Indonesian female performer" with a (sometimes unrecognized) sense of feminist praxis. Here, women's long-standing subordination, as framed by state patriarchy, can be challenged—albeit often in veiled or coded ways—through artistic agency.

Experience versus Indoctrinated Memory: Methodology as Experimental Method

This book is first and foremost based on my long-term practice of many of the dances discussed within, which fall into the two main state-designated categories of folk dance and court dance. Although at first my learning process was kept hidden from public view, I studied these forms during my childhood, growing up in an East Javanese village where I was trained through the traditional transmission of practice, a local system that nonetheless has a gender- and class-based genealogy and carries a sense of ownership and pride. I continued studying both categories as part of my higher education, mostly learning dances that were associated with the dominant forms of state representation and therefore highly appreciated within the world of official culture and attractive to international consumers, including those in U.S. academia. In addition to dance training, my alliances with the Institute of the Arts, first as a student and then, since 1992, as a faculty member, have given me almost unlimited access to official events and palace and state ceremonies. This access has afforded me an intimate view of the exclusionary processes operative within the realm of arts, based on the categories of gender, political alliances, and/or the ethnic background of an artistic practice.

My involvement has also led to invaluable friendships and collaborations with female performers and choreographers, most of whom are trained as court dancers. I am indebted to them for offering me insight and continuing entrée into the space of the practice of royal and national culture, particularly after my own official exit from this sphere following the changes in my geographical location and political alliances. These women have allowed me to more fully understand their firm attachment to the practice of Javanese court dance and Balinese "sacred ritual," which gives them the status of "national treasures" and valorizes their citizenship in the nation-state.

The forms practiced by such artists have long been known as "timeless" and "ancient," yet many have elements that are easily identifiable as bearing Dutch colonial influence, as well as later changes introduced during independence, or under the New Order in the process of establishing a common, uniform national aesthetic. My connection to these artists and their work, and my own former alliances with the state arts system, have allowed me to bridge the discrete yet converging worlds of government apparatus and cultural practice and enabled me to inhabit a location—although certainly not unproblematically— that provokes the theoretical possibility of exploiting a certain "flexibility" in my citizenship, which in some ways has increased with my immersion in the academic world outside of Indonesia.

My own rare opportunities for experimentation that have enriched this book are in a large part due to my role as a Ford Foundation and an American Association of University Women grantee. This funding (in combination with my lengthy "residence" within Western academia) has enabled me to explore, create, and produce both research and performances with less state intervention or control than is normally possible for Indonesian scholars. (The foreign institutions of course also have their own rules and agendas, the specifics of which I address in later chapters.)

As Edward Said stated about his own work: "I have tried to maintain a critical consciousness as well as employing those instruments of historical, humanistic, and cultural research of which my education has made me the fortunate beneficiary."[45] Inspired by the

work of Said and others, I have also used the space of border crossing and education abroad to remove myself from my active role as an
Indonesian civil servant, educator, and female artist, attempting to
view the complex social and political environment that surrounds
me as reflected from a place "outside."

The process has afforded me room to temporarily avoid the direct gaze of the Indonesian government and the absolute inevitabil-
ity of its intervention, as I have sought to explore the possibilities of
this new space, to see if it was really "true," that it might at some
level enable me to write, choreograph, and—borrowing Geoffrey
Robinson's words—"run against a heavy tide of scholarly and popular opinion."[46] Yet much of the published, *scholarly* opinion I seek to
challenge in fact hails from the same space to which I have "escaped,"
and furthermore is deeply rooted in the direct and indirect complicity of generations of Western "Indonesianists" with the authority of
the New Order state.

Thus, despite the many important new allies acquired, I have in
some ways traded in one Big Brother only to realize I am in the den
of another, which at times has come to seem quite frightening itself.
Yet I am driven by my family, my history, my curiosity, and my attachment to the world of dance production and practice in Indonesia,
which has embedded in me a strong desire to understand the ever-
shifting mixture of the historical, cultural, political, and personal,
vying for dominance and expression in the space that exists between
dance practice and the distribution of power and control.

2. WHAT IS LEFT

The Fabricated and the Illicit

> Saina told the investigating team that she participated in a "dirty, indecent dance, the dance of the 'Fragrant Flowers' which was performed nakedly everyday, both during the day and at night. The 400 men present would watch 200 women, after which free sex would occur, in which every woman sometimes had to serve three or four men sexually."[1]

This quotation is the "confession" of Saina, a seventeen-year-old identified by a military newspaper in 1965 as a member of Gerwani (the acronym for "Gerakan Wanita Indonesia," or "Indonesian Women's Movement"), a progressive women's association that was later banned by Suharto. In the official state narrative of the events in question, Gerwani was held partially responsible for the death and alleged torture of six Army generals and one high-ranking officer on September 30, 1965; its members were suspected of being communist sympathizers who had participated in special revolutionary training. As Saskia Wieringa argues in her book, these kinds of descriptions were produced in order to establish extreme anti-communist sentiments within Indonesian society, simultaneously making convenient scapegoats of Gerwani members[2]—who were already highly unpopular with much of the patriarchal establishment—by associating them with the killing of the seven officers. Meanwhile, a blind eye was turned to the mass murders perpetrated across the country by the military, as it was to the support and participation in the murders of several civilian groups.

In this chapter, I examine how post-massacre cultural reconstruction in Indonesia has been a form of domination, mobilized to maintain control over cultural identity formation, and by extension both domestic order and international relations. I focus on how state narratives surrounding the 1965–66 massacres were reproduced in society through the fabrication of memory. I argue that this tactic primarily affected, and in various ways continues to affect, those bodies that were viewed as unruly for political reasons and were thus made into convenient, corporeal symbols of the ongoing "evil" against which the New Order claimed its legitimacy as protector and representative of the idealized nation.

I also analyze the political connections between state narratives and the "voluntary" cooperation of the populace. Taking Benedict Anderson's analysis of nationalism in relation to Western imperialism as an important point of departure,[3] I seek to show that the New Order's particular approach—combining very specifically sculpted "remembrances" of a national past with a massively enforced forgetting of actual historical experience—cannot possibly provide true reconciliation or healing for those victimized. Rather, that which may be remembered and that which must be forgotten—the sequence and importance of certain events—has simply been edited in an attempt to shape and guide consciousness and public memory on a national level.

This strategy is meant to direct individual members of society in their understanding of the past—most crucially the *recent* past and the events of 1965—where passed time has essentially been extracted from the progression of history and returned to citizens as "ours" only after its reconstruction by the government. As Indonesians, then, the version of the massacres we *must* remember is the centralized and founding narrative created by the state; recalling or narrating events as they transpired and were experienced would perhaps be tantamount to blocking out or forgetting the state itself. Conversely, if the legitimacy of the state is recognized, then the death and imprisonment of citizens that enabled Suharto's New Order regime to take control of the nation are erased from view or forgotten. In order to create a selective amnesia toward the facts of history, then, the state has produced its own narration of the past through various media: film, educational curricula, museum exhibits, sculpture, and, perhaps most ubiquitously, the "traditional" performing arts.

Politics of Memory: Body and the Disciplining of Alliance

We are standing in lines, grouped by grade, stretching many rows back. Each group has a supervising teacher and one older student assigned to lead them. We are hot and sweaty in our nylon and polyester uniforms, but we are used to standing like that during our frequent training for baris berbaris, *or marching in line, which is meant to instill discipline and provide physical exercise. This particular march takes us into town, walking carefully in different rhythmic patterns while the leader shouts at us, imitating the familiar call of the Army sergeants:* satu, dua, tiga! *(one, two, three!). On the street we pass many honking cars, buses, and trucks, showing their support and approval. We are marching to celebrate* Kesaktian Pancasila *on October 1, which the government has declared a day to commemorate the strength of the nation and its freedom. The freedom we are honoring, however, is not our independence from the Dutch or the Japanese, but our "liberation" from what the government officials call* Pengkhianatan G30S–PKI, *or "The Treason of the September 30th Movement and the Communist Party (PKI)," words indoctrinated by the state, which all children must learn in class.*

The marching, street parade, and uniforms are adapted to culturally represent each region and school; the event is thus turned into a "cultural" performance competition, judged on variations, complexity and synchronicity of steps, combinations of movements, costume design, and songs. The competition and creative participation—albeit in a highly predefined context—function to drum up enthusiasm among students such as myself, giving it the feel of a special event in which we are personally invested rather than a mere civic obligation. Every year on October 1 we also go to a small local theater to see the film bearing the same title as the government slogan: Pengkhianatan G30S–PKI.[4] *Again and again the film "showed" us the PKI's evil betrayal of our young nation, fixing and embedding the words from our history textbooks—which form the state's version of the events leading up to the mass killings in 1965—with explicit, graphic, and melodramatic imagery. Viewing is mandatory, and each student would single out and memorize different scenes, depending on which part he or she would chose to describe in a report that was always assigned the next day in class. I preferred to focus on the dancing scenes, especially those parts accompanied by singing, that often showed forbidden art forms that we were allowed to see only by viewing the film at this special time of year.*

The women in this cinematic narrative—created by a special team under the Ministries of Education and Defense and the military—are portrayed as bloodthirsty, sexualized extremists.[5] These brutal sexual politics, repeated and reproduced throughout the media and national education systems, have constituted the dominant ideological force in the construction and establishment of a widespread Indonesian collective memory. This phenomenon includes the portrayal of women who take active roles in voicing their sociopolitical concerns and making themselves seen and heard in the form of street protests. In the film, the image of such women is reconfigured through a pointedly arranged scene. In it, a military wife's activism and membership in political organizations are presented in stark opposition to the longing of her husband and children for her comforting, feminine presence in the domestic space of the home. Like other socially, politically active women in the film, the woman's "low" moral character is signified by the then-modern look: short hair and a skirt hemmed high enough to walk comfortably while keeping in stride with men. Through similarities in wardrobe, the politically involved wife and mother is thus visually equated with those other "liberal" women believed to have taken revenge—in the form of torture, mutilation, and castration—on the bodies of prominent, dominant men: Gerwani. The clear implication was that all wives, mothers, or daughters actively participating in shaping the conditions of their own sociocultural surrounds—whether rural or cosmopolitan, informal or overtly political—potentially constituted a grave threat to national morality and domestic patriarchal order.

The watching of the film, particularly its required viewing by schoolchildren, was embedded like a centerpiece in a specially tailored journey through national history lasting several days. On the mornings following the screening, the teachers, especially those who taught us PSPB (*Pelajaran Sejarah Perjuangan Bangsa,* or Study of the History of the National Struggle) and P4 (*Pedoman Penghayatan Pengamalan Pancasila,*[6] Course on Guidelines Embodying *Pancasila* [The Five Principles of Indonesian Citizenship]) would review the details of the film, drawing parallels between its cinematic realism and the pages of our textbooks. From their precise, "empirical" lectures, we learned, again, exactly what we needed to remember about the rebirth of our proud nation, including the identities, roles, and qualities of all the major and minor characters, heroes, and villains.

From the time of the event until now, more than forty years later, the narrative journey has stood its ground remarkably well, despite the subsequent fall of its most heroic protagonist from power and from any semblance of grace. Suharto's resignation amid heavy protests in 1998 has perhaps been taken as a separate episode of the same, longer story: a tragedy in which the dictator falls, and yet the nation, and its history, remain still as promised. The perspective of the millions who were imprisoned or murdered post–September 30, 1965, has never been given official space for expression, nor has evidence been brought to public light of who is to blame for their deaths. Their lives cannot be returned, and many of the children they left behind remain in a state of confusion as to the fate of their parents and the true significance of their loss.

In *Imagined Communities,* Benedict Anderson elucidates the "strange habit" of European colonizers' frequent construction of a "new version" of their existing capitals on occupied territories—as in New York, New London, New Amsterdam, or "Nouvelle Orleans." Anderson sees this practice as historically similar to the earlier, intraregional renaming of Asian cities such as Chiangmai (New City) in Thailand or Kota Baru (New Town) in Central Java. In the latter instances, he argues that the claiming of a "new" often functioned to signify a succession, inheritance, or geographical shift in the locus of regional power, as if the "old" had vanished and been replaced: "'new' and 'old' are aligned diachronically, and the former appears always to invoke an ambiguous blessing from the dead." In the case of the Europeans, however, what is indicated is an expansion, rather than a shift in the locus of power. There, the "'new' and 'old' were understood synchronically, co-existing within homogeneous, empty time."[7]

In my analysis, the rise of Suharto and the renaming of Indonesia's ruling elite as the "New Order" (causing Sukarno's ousted regime to be referred to as the "Old Order") accomplished *both* of Anderson's versions of the transfer of power simultaneously. The establishment of the New Order signified a shift in the locus of control as the mantle of president was diachronically passed down, or "inherited," by Suharto; yet through the reconstruction and foregrounding of Indonesia's "timeless culture," the new leader conjured his synchronic existence in *parallel* with the mythical status of the Javanese royal hierarchy, located at a remove in the Central Javanese city of Yogyakarta, where the sultan has "always" held court. Even the deposed leader of *Orde Lama* (the "Old Order"), Sukarno, continued to "exist" as a now-ghostly, yet irreplaceable, icon of independent nationhood, mutely haunting the capital city under house arrest until his death in 1970 (and thereafter in the still-ubiquitous, legendary images of his defiant heyday).[8] Thus the Suharto regime systematized the establishment and legitimacy of its own rule by engendering specific patterns of memory and forgetting, inserting itself in a new, yet "time-honored" national identity reconstructed by the state following its rise to power.

Through this fabricated memory, the state restructured not only national history but also the cultural identity of certain groups, in particular the politically active women mentioned previously, by making connections between their cultural activities of dancing and singing and barbaric or abusive behaviors that flouted the norms by which female citizens of Indonesia are typically expected to behave. This reconstructed identity was applied to women who were involved in organizations and activities that, during the events of 1965, were suddenly deemed illegal and swiftly banned. One might say that their activities were transformed retroactively into a mark of deviance in order to justify, post facto, the harsh treatment they received. Women who were targeted included those with purported links to the PKI (membership in almost any left-leaning or Sukarnoist group, including organizations with no direct affiliation whatsoever with the PKI, also came to serve as sufficient evidence of "contamination" by leftist ideals), those who provided friendship or assistance to a Communist Party member, or those who were married or related, even distantly, to a party member. Such citizens, whether involved in a direct or tertiary way, were officially stigmatized by the application of the label *tidak bersih lingkungan,* or "unclean environment." This powerful defamation thus turned those who had been cast out—many of their bodies, and the traces they left behind, had both physically and ideologically "disappeared"—into political and social outcasts.

The state defended its violent actions by claiming they were necessary in order to maintain peace and national security. They further mobilized these concepts to codify and legalize both the guidelines for civil conduct and the duties of good citizens as well as to establish procedures for state action to be taken against those who fell outside of these newly marked boundaries. Behavior that was officially labeled "subversive" was not limited to direct participation in communism or public dissent but included any act that might be construed as indirect involvement, assistance, or fraternization with those considered in violation of social and political norms and therefore in opposition to the government. Both direct and indirect involvement with such groups was viewed as a political crime, known as *terlibat* ("implicated"), or simply as a "subversive act."

In this way, the identities of Gerwani members and other female political activists who were victims of the New Order were taken—often along with their bodies—and hidden or destroyed, then reconstructed and finally presented to the public in their subverted forms.[9] Instead of being viewed as victims of the New Order and its military oppression, then, because of state propaganda and official history, such women have been framed as citizens who knowingly committed a grave error, and, if they were "lucky" enough to have remained alive, must now struggle nationally, locally, and even within their own families to be seen once more as potentially useful members of society. Through photos, film, news media, and doctrines in public meetings and educational curricula, this reconstructed identification of progressive or artistically oriented female citizenship cohered, creating a body of reference within national and international understanding that came to be considered a valid resource.

Because it was important for the state to portray itself in a favorable light in order to construct the consent of the public through control of collective memory, it defended its claims of the necessity of exterminating the PKI while paradoxically avoiding admission of any kind of responsibility for the mass killings that had occurred. If people revealed memories of the event that differed from the state narratives, they too were categorized as subversive or anti-nationalist and silenced through various repressive state apparatus. The blame for such actions was consistently placed on the victims, who were accused of betraying their own country.

In this context, people suspected or categorized as communist, either with connections to the party or members of Gerwani, *Baperki* or *Badan Permusyawaratan Kewarganegaraan Indonesia* (a Chinese association in Indonesia), BTI (a farmers' association), or SOBSI (a labor union) all became scapegoats, even though they were not necessarily Communist Party members. This entire, large group of citizens was then considered socially, politically, and legally suspect in the extreme.[10] Benedict Anderson called the military's reports of sexual atrocities committed by Gerwani members on behalf of the PKI "icy lies . . . planned to create an anti-Communist hysteria in all strata of Indonesian society."[11] Despite a few strong outside critiques, however, the fabricated knowledge surrounding the events of 1965 was in large part successfully transformed into the dominant narrative, as differing accounts were suppressed. This imposed, self-serving historiography was then supported by books published by the New Order and was immediately added to the national educational curriculum, the production of which was centralized in Jakarta. Under this policy, by the early 1980s, the content of obligatory core courses in national history from first grade through university level was focused on 1965, providing an ever-more detailed political analysis from the state's perspective.

This massive, tightly woven historical tapestry, tactically designed to affect local and national perceptions of the events of 1965, also ultimately skewed international conceptions of, and responses to, the rise of the New Order, despite the criticisms leveled by Robinson, Anderson, and others. According to Dwyer and Santikarma, whose work focuses on the effects of 1965 in Bali, the state's claims that the heavy killings there in particular were based on localized cultural tendencies were also quickly picked up on by foreign reporters: "Most western news accounts of the time tended to strangely echo these claims by the state that the violence was a product of the uncontrollable masses, describing Indonesians slaughtering each other in a mad frenzy, betraying their cultural propensity for falling into mass trance or running amok or simply demonstrating their Third World savagery."[12]

With much of the international political and academic community either lauding or simply ignoring the actions of the Indonesian state and their widespread effects, Suharto was able to operate with relative efficiency and impunity, without the threat of international sanctions or censure. Domestically, those whom Suharto had targeted during his rise to power became known as "Illicit Citizens": a threatening, destructive force continually working against statehood, against the development of nationalism, peace, and religious strength—everything that by national norms constitutes the category of "human"—and thereby necessitating the presence of a vigilant, authoritarian state. Furthermore, the actions of such "leftists" were portrayed as severely tarnishing the honor of Indonesian women, and the particular slander of "betraying women's honor" was used, bolstered by the salacious rumors of the fate of the murdered generals, to convince other women's organizations to turn against Gerwani in favor of alliance with the military; the portrayal of Gerwani women as "liberated" and sexually loose also convinced many Islamic and Christian associations to turn against them.[13] In this way, the New Order's strategies to promote nationalism functioned to build the imaginative "unity" of Indonesia through killing, slandering, and scapegoating certain groups in order to establish an absolute, collective "moral" and legal code that would sacralize the legitimacy of the new state.

Within this strategy, the construction of new "traditional" dance forms or the reconstruction of old ones constituted an important element of the government's effort to represent itself in the international arena. More recently, this practice has also led to the expansion of the symbolic role of dance traditions in strategies aimed at increasing foreign support for economic development and national security programs.

This practice, however, is not necessarily "new." As Matthew Cohen has shown in his richly detailed work on the history of Javanese and Balinese performing arts, contemporary Indonesian cultural/historical memory is in fact quite short.[14] Thus the New Order discourse of channeling the "ancient" Javanese artistic past—a realm of tradition claimed to have been barely touched by the long ravages of history—of course fails to "remember" that artistic change has consistently followed the diverse cultural, economic, and religious *ex*change that Java has always engaged in. The exploiting, colonizing Europeans (whose full-to-bursting museums provide much of the contemporary evidence of historical Indonesian contact with outsiders) were relative latecomers to this process, following millennia of local trade with other parts of Asia as well as the entrance of Hinduism from India, bringing with it, among many other things, the *Ramayana* and *Mahabharata* epics that continue to figure hugely into what is now referred to as "traditional Indonesian dance."

According to Cohen, the first record of European interest in Javanese cultural practice was made after the rise of Islam (which occurred largely through the peaceful influence of Arab and Indian merchants) and describes a 1580 meeting between Javanese and European traders, mediated by an exchange of music sent drifting across the waters between the "native" orchestra of Raja Donan and the musically inclined crew aboard the anchored boat of Francis Drake.[15] While for Cohen, Javanese and Balinese (or later "East Indies") artistic practice has, unlike those of certain other Asian cultures, been consistently valued as catalyst for interest, attraction, and profitable exchange with a vast variety of "foreign" entities and powers, it is for precisely this reason that the arts have undergone a continuous process of change, and, depending on one's perspective, "dilution," since the beginning of recorded time.

Thus, the heightening of European interest in the arts of the Javanese palace in the late nineteenth century (roughly the middle of a period during which "the Indies" were an officially nationalized colony) ushered in both new opportunities for artists to travel and perform abroad and a "period of hyper-development of dance, music and theatre in the central Javanese royal courts of Surakarta and Yogyakarta."[16] The New Order (and contemporary) emphasis on the use of "ancient" traditional arts in the context of diplomacy and international economic interests, then, is in many ways a mirroring of past practice that nonetheless obscures the reality of historical change. The "cultural night abroad," state cultural missions, artist exchanges, and the inclusion of Indonesian forms in European and U.S. curricula are now the result of the "new" policy of exporting culture as a major element of the nation-state's self-promotion on the global political and economic stage. The uncanny presence of centuries-old Javanese and Balinese musical instruments, masks, and dance costumes tucked away in the dark corners of many of the less-recently explored European archives, however, marks only the beginning of a potentially endless historical voyage of discovery that for me has both continued and begun with the ability to travel provided by interest in dance.

Misi Kesenian and *Bedhaya*: Femininized Power and Dancing Myth

Misi Kesenian or "arts mission" (also sometimes called *Misi Kebudayaan* or "cultural mission") is a term used in Indonesia to refer to state-administered performances of traditional arts, presented abroad for various official events and functions, including the promotion of foreign policy and international goodwill, the honoring of government guests, the opening of new embassies, the development of new trade relations, and the exchange of arts faculty or visiting or resident artists. Typically, such cultural missions feature Javanese or Balinese ritual or court-based dance forms, which have been given the highest status and most attention within state cultural reconstruction.

Under Suharto, the intense efforts to ban and vilify certain art forms while skillfully promoting and funding others for development slowly sculpted the nation-state's new identity in the form of a basic set of fixed cultural expressions available for local, national, and global distribution and consumption. As the arts became a major component in the promotion of the Indonesian state in global communications, the state simultaneously redefined "the arts"—and the apparent tastes of Indonesian artists and audiences—in alignment with its domestic ideological needs and its reading of the global cultural market. In this process of transformation, the "contents" of many existing dances were often reinterpreted in terms of more mythical frameworks, in which they were given an apparently ritual or religious value, and standardized under the refined concepts of Javanese court artistry. In the years following 1965, the continuing standardization and nationalization of culture by the New Order indeed appeared to be popular with most civilians. However, artists' and patrons' expressions of approval or support for such policies were often necessarily entangled with their own defensive efforts to erase or disclaim their histories of alignment with certain groups or institutions now banned under the *bersih lingkungan,* or clean environment policy of the New Order.[17]

These blanket policies, however, had far less relevance for artists in the palace and courts because the royal hierarchy and the Javanese high court culture were believed to be inherently ideologically opposed to the communist agenda, due to the fact that court dance, known for mythologizing the power of the Javanese king or promoting the ideal of a refined and aristocratic female, seemed solidly anti-proletarian. The fear that the arts of the Javanese palace might be promoting proletarian values simply never materialized; in fact, the mythical stature of Javanese kings has been strongly promoted since the massacres in 1965–66, and many of the written *kejawen,* or Javanese myths, have served as a resource for new, state-approved repertoires.

It would seem that Suharto's New Order was attracted to the *kejawen* because it found an affinity with the aristocratic power structure of these stories. Accordingly, the Javanese court dances chosen for reconstruction were often those understood as representing a symbolic centralization of the power of the king, in an attempt to draw connections between the current government—with Suharto as "monarch"—and the mythic powers of past rulers. Javanese dance also manifests the symbolic power of the current king of Yogyakarta, in Central Java (after independence from the Dutch, several regional kings retained representative positions as cultural figureheads), and the "orderliness" of the kingdom, symbolized by the refinement of danced expression, slow movements, flowing, soft *gamelan* music, and chanting. Although it is normally only performed at top-level diplomatic meetings amid appropriately refined settings, *Bedhaya* (pronounced "Bedoyo"), a Javanese court dance practiced solely by women, is considered to be the ideal model for state missions, as it foregrounds both the aesthetic of "ancient" palace rituals and the (now state-employed) women who once occupied the role of courtesans to the kings.

The dance itself describes the mythical relationship between the king of Java and the supernatural forces said to emanate from the spirit Nyai Lara Kidul (the queen of the South Sea), and the Abode of the Dead, where she resides. The movements symbolize the union of the king's power with that of the underworld, when the goddess-queen of the South Sea becomes his consort; as a result of this coalition, the king is believed to be imbued with the power to rule over the country (formerly Java, or parts of Java, and the various other islands and provinces under its control). If we focus on the ritualistic relationship between the king and his mythical ocean queen as represented in Javanese dances such as *Bedhaya* and *Srimpi* (a less complex version of *Bedhaya* that is frequently performed on culture missions), the king appears to possess a potent authority over the realm of the sea; in this context, the water can be seen as a symbol for an omnipresent, all-encompassing, and natural structure of power.

In addition to the established *kejawen* and choreographic adaptations, the New Order in fact commissioned a few "new" works from the palace, although still in Javanese court style, that describe the fight for independence and revere Suharto's role as a national hero, making rather obvious allusions to his status as the new king of Java/Indonesia, and to his alignment with the omniscient, mythical power of the sultan. Since their inauguration in the early New Order years, these "historical" dances have been taught at many arts institutes, colleges, and high schools as a part of the core curriculum in national culture and tradition. *Bedhaya,* however, is always referenced as the "original" palace form and thus the most important and valuable as a symbol of national cultural heritage; according to many Javanese court dancers, the queen of the South can "appear" during a *Bedhaya* performance, called forth by the representation of her spiritual-political relationship with the once-powerful king of Central Java.[18]

As the second most common Island-based tradition within national cultural representation, Balinese performance also sometimes reflects the court context and former political might of Balinese kingdoms, but it more often relates to temple practices that when performed in a ritual context are said to facilitate communication with Balinese Hindu gods who must be placated and served. Occasionally, Sumatran dances are also performed on state culture missions, but usually only when the Indonesian ambassador or embassy representative in the target country is from Sumatra. For example, in the 1994 mission to Vietnam, after the Javanese offerings, the Indonesian government troupe also performed *Rantak,* a West Sumatran dance, and *Saman,* an Acehnese dance and chant. Although in that year the political situation in Aceh was extremely volatile as a result of an ongoing struggle between a local secession movement and government troops, no mention of the situation there was made during the mission; the focus, as per state policy, was on highly visible events and encounters, furthering information, which, although deeply political in nature, was disguised in a translucent veil of "culture."

In the case of Javanese court and Balinese temple dance, these practices are still frequently deployed on state missions because their long-term foregrounding on the international stage has led to their renown as visually spectacular and aesthetically pleasing in terms of both movement and costume as well as musical accompaniment. These dances, then, are thought to increase the prestige and status of the Indonesian state within the larger community of nations. Accordingly, the government considers (and requires) its performing artists to be official diplomatic representatives, charged with the important task of embodying the symbolic "face" of the state, aesthetically mediating its commerce and exchange with Indonesia's most powerful allies on the global stage.

The artists, then, and the special "missions" they execute, function to legitimize the state, conveying subtly packaged yet essential ideological meanings that symbolically construct the significance of Indonesia according to a set of rigid cultural codes. Because of the crucial diplomatic role they play, the artists and their affiliated in-stitutions (that is, national schools of the arts, conservatories, artists' associations, and so on) are carefully chosen and closely controlled by the Indonesian state through detailed written doctrines and strict rules of conduct. In addition, the individual dance numbers chosen to be performed abroad are further revised in a number of ways to make them more amenable, or "appropriate," for large foreign audi-ences. At the very least, they are taken out of their usual context, be it at the palace or temple, and presented as staged events that aim to impress and capture the interest of large groups of non-Indonesians. Official state rhetoric, as well as that of affiliated private art insti-tutions, emphasizes the missions' fostering of cross-cultural under-standing; more realistically, such missions emphasize and exploit the well-established "ancient" and "exotic" status of local performance traditions in order to draw international tourists to Indonesia and satisfy the multiculturalist agendas of the missions' host countries. When performed domestically, centrally regulated national culture in many ways has a similar effect: that of the ideological transfor-mation of Indonesian citizens into touristic consumers of their own traditions in a highly controlled, museum-like environment.[19]

The Ritual: *Bedhaya* and the Imaginary King

Suluk, *a type of chanting using the higher vocal registers, is begun by a* Dalang, *who conducts the music ensemble and directs the dance called* Bedhaya. *His chant breaks the silence in the court pavil-ion, followed by* gendhing *(a type of musical arrangement for the gamelan orchestra), guiding the dancers' movements. His hand starts beating the* keprak *(a percussive instrument consisting of a specially designed hardwood box) with the sound* thro thok thok, thro thok thok. *One by one the dancers kneeling on the floor of the sul-tan's pavilion are led to center stage by two old women, positioning them directly in front of the king's throne. The senior women are in charge of fixing and maintaining the dancers' costumes and ap-pearances while on stage, making sure they are presented properly, with skirts always covering their legs so as not to disturb the refined elegance of the ritual.*

The dancers get up slowly, make a line, and stand straight, their left hands holding a corner of their skirts, defining a wide arc that hangs below the arm, like a flag. The skirts are decorated with special, hand-drawn batik that supposedly marks class association, visually linking the dancers to royal society. Gold and diamonds on their hands show the elegance of their bodies decorated with accessories, glamorized corporeality on the dance floor. The king sits poised in his chair at the front of the pavilion, his costume also quite elaborate.[20] Behind him, many guests and servants sit very upright and still, causing me to have difficulty breathing as I watch from behind the door, although I am not even dancing that night. Observing the performance from the audience, with its highly ritualized movements and sacred symbolism, I wonder if my menstruation is the reason I am forbidden to perform even the role of emban (a helper on stage during the performance). Or perhaps I had simply fallen out of favor with those defining the intricate politics of control and display underneath the apparently smooth and refined exterior of the Keraton palace, Indonesia's primary symbol of its ancient "mythical" heritage and "modern" national culture.

The dancers walk slowly, in synch with the keprak combined with the sounds of the Dutch cornet. Marching one by one, their bodies are properly disciplined and controlled, seeming to have the same height and weight. I praise their self-restraint highly, as do the other members of the audience that night. The dance, as always, is so slow, yet no one sleeps.

While this version of *Bedhaya* is generally considered too "sacred" to leave the context of the palace (and is therefore rare even on state culture missions), on a few occasions, similar performances have nonetheless been held abroad in nondiplomatic contexts, such as the Los Angeles Festival in 1990.[21] There, however, the effect seemed quite different: after the performance, the musicians reported that much of the audience had in fact dozed off. While preparations for the trip were also beset by myriad disagreements, such as who would take the position of leader of the group during the tour and who would stay in which hotel room, the troupe nonetheless returned home proudly, having experienced a rare (for dancers who mainly perform inside the Yogyakarta palace) trip to the United States.

Domestically, in 1988, I also witnessed a complete *Bedhaya* performance that was held at the Presidential Palace in Jakarta by the same dancers and musicians; there as well, no Javanese king was present. Presiding in his place, however, was Suharto, the reigning dictator. In this context, then, the (dis)placement of *Bedhaya* was a conscious shift, and, accordingly, this event and the performances for the king appeared nearly identical in terms of corporeal layout and conception. The music also skillfully mimicked the gamelan of the sultan's palace, and as in that context, the marching and the sound of the cornet reminded me how profoundly the Dutch were able to influence the Javanese king's choice of music to accompany the female dancers.

Performance of *Bedhaya Sumreg,* created by the king of Yogyakarta Hamengkubuwono I (1755–92), at the Yogyakarta Palace. The narrative is centered on the meeting of the sultan of Yogyakarta by the queen of the South Sea (a mystical and mythological figure) in response to the separation of the Mataram kingdom (which was split into the Yogyakarta and Surakarta palaces in 1755). Photographer/copyright: Himawan.

Observing the scene, I was drawn into memories of the training in body movement and control that I, like the women performing in front of me, had undergone since I was very young in a variety of different contexts. As a child, the European elements in Javanese mysticism, which infused and informed our daily practice, were taken as obvious and natural, as if they had always been a part of that which we were learning to do: to symbolize the "effortless" unity of our heritage.

Cultural Policy: Flashback

Prior to 1965, Sukarno promoted national cultural policy to build and develop the young country "on its own terms." During his reign as president, cultural construction was based on what is known in Indonesia as the "unification of ideas," which referred to and drew upon the cooperation of many different ethnic and cultural practices, assembled in order to strengthen a new and distinct Indonesian national identity in opposition and resistance to colonial and imperial influences. Under Sukarno, then, dance narratives were not necessarily representative of an ethnically centralized agenda, in the sense that Javanisation and Balinisation were not the only dominant priorities in cultural policy. Rather, from independence until 1965, there was a greater sense of flexibility in the representation of tradition and frequently an emphasis on the use of a variety of "everyday" (non–palace-affiliated) practices to represent local cultures.[22]

The influence of European theater was present as well, alongside folk or village-based performances and the "high" culture of the palace. During that time, among many other forms, folk dances such as *Gandrung, Tayub,* and *Jathilan* and other popular performing arts such as *Kethoprak* (a famously raucous and satirical form of traditional theater from East and Central Java), *Ludruk* (East Java traditional theater), and *Gambuh* (Balinese theater) were produced in many different contexts and at local, regional, and national levels.

At that time artists and performers were not nationalized through induction as civil servants, and there were no *pembinaan,* the official domestic arts missions to rural areas. (*Pembinaan* were aimed at information gathering and at retraining and "improving" village performers according to official guidelines.) With the strong presence in the 1950s and early '60s of so many different political parties competing in each region for membership, many performers split their association between two or more groups with differing ideologies. Both the communist PKI and the right-leaning, nationalist PNI (Partai Nasionalis Indonesia) attracted numerous members throughout the nation. A large percentage of both rural and urban artists were also involved in Lekra (the People's Cultural Association), an arts guild that offered both support and a commitment to helping members, and the general public, with a wide range of daily necessities.[23] In the more open and varied political environment of the Sukarno years,[24] many artists also performed at functions for both of the major political parties without being members of either. Popular artists or art forms were employed at rallies and events because of their proven ability to draw and hold the attention of large crowds, and thus arts production at the village and national levels played a significant role in the representation of political alliances, especially with the growing competition between the two major parties (PNI and PKI).

In the early years of Sukarno's presidency many theater and performance groups also made use of Western, and especially European, influences. With the Cold War, however, came changes, many of which were aimed at instilling a national opposition to the perceived emptiness and moral corruption of the West, and particularly American culture. Yet since before independence, many local art forms were influenced by the global ubiquity of European style and thus had frequently become less concerned with attachment to the expression of any particular local ethnic group. For example, the group Dardanella, formed in the late Dutch era, claimed members from many different ethnic and geographic backgrounds within the archipelago and performed widely in both cities and villages. During the late colonial years, the Japanese occupation during World War II, and the early Sukarno years, Dardanella (along with many of its members, who became famous performers in their own right) was able to represent a varied, local character without focusing on royalty or myth[25]—its representations were not dependent on the symbolism of the Javanese high court. For such artists, this disengagement from specific ethnic codes resulted in a greater sense of openness and possibility in the creation of performing arts, which at the time was also generally detached from fear regarding appropriate content. Unknown to its practitioners at the time, such "universal" art would also provide relative discursive distance from suspicions of having harbored proletarian concerns or promoted class awareness, which would become sensitive and deadly issues post-1965.[26]

Although clearly, such liberating detachment came from the connection to or the embracement of a style considered more European, still, Dardanella's choices enabled it to gradually move away from the central position of Java while continuing to exist within the general context of domestic ethnic representation. As such, it also gained the opportunity to tour other Asian countries such as Burma/Myanmar, China, Hong Kong, Singapore, and India, and then further extended their presence to Europe and the United States.[27]

However, for postindependence diplomatic occasions hosted by Sukarno, such as the visits of Ho Chi Minh or other political leaders to Indonesia, the performances often featured Balinese dance, staged in the Istana Tampak Siring Bali (the presidential house in Bali). Also, many groups from the Javanese court were sent on delegations, especially to Holland, and Balinese groups were sent to Russia as well as to other European countries and the United States. There was, however, no clear official document guiding these choices; the state policy regarding what may be considered an "Indonesian" art form did not directly address issues of Javanisation or Balinisation, although these trends and strategies were obviously being practiced in parallel with many others.[28] It was not until the violent arrival of "regime change" in 1965 that the state began a concerted, nationwide effort to unify and control Indonesian cultural arts according to a rigidly defined framework.

Before the New Order came to power, Sukarno's political stance and policies, which initially legalized all political parties and youth associations, both religious and secular, worked in concert with his openness to non-court culture within national representation, especially to alternative "traditional" forms of Indonesian arts practice. At the same time, however, mindful of how he wished to represent his country abroad and how foreign societies might influence Indonesians of certain classes, particularly those who were young and impressionable, he maintained a very specific—and certainly not unproblematic—idea of what distinguished Western culture from Eastern culture.

Following from this, Sukarno began to probe the possibility of a new relationship with China, building economic and mercantile cooperation and determining other common interests. In the context of the Cold War, this potential alliance served to heighten the U.S. alarm over the spread of communism in Southeast Asia, which was compounded by the significant membership of Indonesia's Communist Party, despite the nation's status as a noncommunist "democratic" republic. Theodore Friend puts the PKI membership in 1965 at a massive 27 million—the largest such entity in any country without a formal communist government.[29]

Even before then, by 1957, the United States was concerned about the strength of the PKI as well as the young nation's robust policy of political and economic resistance to the West under the leadership of Sukarno. Sukarno's willingness to allow Communist Party representation alongside Islamic and other nationalist political parties (the largest of which was the PNI) produced a stern, critical reaction from the United States. Local opponents of the left, primarily Islamic conservative groups and those factions of the military under Suharto's influence, also opposed the government's openness to political diversity and thus became key agents in the eventual restructuring of Indonesia post-1965. Toward the end of Sukarno's presidency, as economic difficulty developed and political chaos began to emerge, opposing sides of national disputes were gradually brought into rough alignment with the international Cold War axis, partially influencing the rise of conditions under which Indonesia was subjected to frequent instability and eventual mass violence.[30]

In the two years following 1965, the charismatic Sukarno's near-universal popularity in Indonesia, which had created a strong sense of nationalism throughout his presidency, slowly collapsed as, among other things, the MPRS (Decree of the Provisional People's Consultative Assembly of the Republic of Indonesia) was created under Suharto's influence in opposition to Sukarno's call for national responsibility and due process after the attempted coup on September 30. This loss of confidence in Sukarno was exacerbated by the breakdown of the economy and the widespread influence of the Cold War. With the blame for failing internal and international affairs increasingly placed on Sukarno by the right, the door appeared to be opening for Suharto to stake a claim on leadership of the nation.

The massacres of 1965–66 occurred at the point of greatest public tension between right-wing and left-aligned parties, which also led to the implication of artists and their practices as a kind of populist "weapon" that might be picked up and used by either side. Under the New Order, then, an immediate effort was made to harness the capacity of cultural production and mold it into a dedicated instrument of state power by centralizing administration of the arts under a nationwide system of government authority. Following the waning of Sukarno's popularity and the subsequent intimidation and murder of his allies and followers, Suharto's nationalized policy, distributed through many branches of government, gained the support of large numbers of conservative, nationalist civilians (many of whom carried strong anti-communist beliefs) in favor of "moralizing" dance and other performing arts through homogenization of the representation of aesthetic values and customs. (The policy was also "supported," as mentioned earlier, by many others as a result of state coercion and widespread fear.) The homogenization spread quickly throughout Indonesia, from the village level up to the large arts organizations, which were destroyed, nationalized, or subsumed by state cultural policy under Suharto's New Order.

According to Geoffrey Robinson's detailed analysis of the regulation of culture in Indonesia after 1965, state officials propagated the notion of beauty and sacredness in all aspects of Indonesian life in an attempt to cover up the violence of genocide still fresh in the minds of the populace while promoting the legitimacy of the new government.[31] The purification of the image of the state in association with that of the nation also served to retroactively place blame for the violence that occurred on the PKI, who were depicted as having brought in dangerous, "foreign" ideas such as Marxism and women's rights. With the strong presence of nationalism already well established since independence, the appropriation and construction of a new "special" identity for Indonesia was made synonymous with patriotic duty. The state's policies took hold quickly within the populace, forming a rigid veneer of beauty to cover the vast landscapes of violence, while simultaneously and profoundly dominating the sphere of cultural production within the territory bounded by federalist ideas.

In my understanding of this approach to building nationalism, I depart from Partha Chatterjee's analysis of nationalism as a struggle of colonial exploitation that aims at demonstrating the falsity of colonizer's claims.[32] As an Indian writer, Partha Chatterjee of course examines nationalism from his own location and perspective. Thus, for him, nationalism reveals the falsity of colonizers' claims that "backward" colonial subjects were culturally incapable of ruling themselves under the conditions of the modern world. In this context, the ability of so-called underdeveloped nations to nationalize functioned as an assertive demonstration that they could modernize themselves while retaining their cultural identities. In turn the nationalized populace created "indigenous" discourse that functioned to challenge colonial claims upon which the exercise of political domination was based.

In revealing some of the differences and similarities between India's and Indonesia's histories of colonialism, Chatterjee's analysis has helped me to understand the process of discourse formulation, especially as to how Indonesian nationalism gradually changed its function. In Indonesia, the nationalism that was a means of decolonization and a form of resistance to Western imperialism became entangled with the agenda of Suharto's regime, which incessantly and selectively manipulated such ideas in the process of building the second, "new" postcolonial nation-state, following independence from the Dutch and the subsequent overthrow of Sukarno's left-leaning and emphatically anti-imperial "Old Order."

In this context, the particular structuring of national identity through the manipulation of cultural practices and the privileging of art forms associated with royal lineage and "ancient," established systems of power functioned seamlessly as an ideological support system for the continued economic and political dominance of the ruling class. The end result of cultural reinvention through the reconstruction of the performing arts, and dance in particular, was a unified memory field through which the state also convinced citizens to actively support its agenda of economic development. People were specifically encouraged to participate in this national plan through engaging in officially sanctioned cultural practice and maintaining vigilance over the control of its structure and display.

Within the sphere of Suharto's reign, the effort to sustain the participation of citizenry in performing arts led to the expanded role of dance traditions, the goal being not the welfare of each citizen-practitioner but rather an increase in foreign support for economic development and national security programs. Through the arts, representation of the nation was accomplished from one, hegemonic perspective rather than the various—albeit also sometimes domineering—angles employed in the past. The "cultural night abroad," cultural missions, artist exchanges, and inclusion in European and U.S. curricula were all key elements of the new policy that sought to export culture as part of the nation-state's propaganda and economic stimulus machine.

On-Screen Betrayal: The Fall and Rise of the "Unrefined" Arts

Carried off within the gears of that very machine, exhausted from marching, yet strangely elated at the prospect of "skipping school" to go to the cinema, each year I sit and watch as the screen magically turns from white to red, as the lights are extinguished and all eyes are instinctively drawn to the front of the theater. Women in crimson dresses come in and out of a room, while men hold a political meeting, looking at maps, planning abduction and murder: actresses portraying Gerwani members. They dance in a field, singing and reciting a now-infamous song called "Gendjer-Gendjer,"[33] then, walking slowly, with a blank face that simultaneously conveys and "masks" the will to do harm, one actress raises a hand in which a razor blade is tightly gripped and the horror of official Indonesian history begins. In the haunting image of this woman's cold, expressionless face and in the echoes of the forbidden song, I find a special fascination, a resonant jolt of powerful memories that refuse to become perfectly clear, repelling me yet affixing my eyes to the all-too-familiar ghosts on the screen.

It was surely not just me. This narrative of female political violence infiltrated the lives of Indonesian citizens in myriad ways. The homes of many children such as myself were invaded by rumors of horror and barbaric femininity, forcibly immersing us in a dilemma of memory, of how to understand the film's narrative in which those committing acts of sexual terror against our nation stood for our mothers, our aunties, our grandmothers and dance teachers.

In addition to their gender-based political attack, however, the images call upon and extend familiar, preexisting codes within the coinciding spheres of dance and social standing. For most citizens, the difference in status between court and non-court dance is considered quite marked, often distinguished by the perception of the lack of a quality of "control," which may be indicated both by environment and by the style of physical movements. The *bangsawan,* or high-class royalty, are believed to produce or enjoy dances that are slow, highly symbolic, and performed in a sacred or royal environment such as the *pendopo,* or traditional Javanese pavilion. These dances, then, are very much in—or under—control. Meanwhile, folk dances are often faster, employing "unrefined" movements of the body, and may be enjoyed in a village courtyard or an open field.

Through the use of an outdoor, folk context in the film, the state-aligned producers drew specific correlations between a type of dance, a social class, and progressive politics, connecting them through the group of dancing Gerwani women and corresponding members of the PKI (also pictured dancing), who appeared violent, unrefined, and out of control, and therefore subversive and dangerous. The free expression of the "proletariat," as interconnected with both workers' and women's rights, was thus choreographed as something lethal to the state body and to national stability. As this suggests, the state did not limit its intense scrutiny to those "refined" art forms that would be trotted out at national and international festivals and diplomatic events. Rather, if anything, at times it appeared even *more* concerned with the thousands of forms existing mainly in rural areas and their tens of millions of practitioners.

The Cultural Repercussions of Regime

Because of the highly stratified, bureaucratic organization of Indonesian society—one of the many dubious inheritances from Dutch colonialism—the central government could reach out its spindly arms to minute corners of the archipelago and reshape the choreography, conceptualization, and public practice of rural traditions in ways that at times seemed truly incredible (or, depending on your position, incredibly terrifying). The method of control relied on the general co-optation of citizens and the strategic placement of agents at the local level: a "neighborhood watch" system presided over by the hierarchy of village officials representing the far end of a chain of command leading straight to Jakarta. In this way, the state was able to keep tabs on the myriad rural "folk" artists who often practiced and performed after returning from work in the fields. Under the New Order's Big Brother–like system, which kept close watch on citizens but largely ignored the mistreatment of civilians by middle- and low-level officials, innumerable injustices and human rights abuses occurred with great regularity throughout the country (*this,* perhaps, was the way a majority of Indonesians experienced the government's much touted "unity in diversity"). Accordingly, the region in which I grew up, in a village in East Java not far from the city of Malang, was no different:

> In December 1965, there was an evening of celebration commemorating the inauguration of a village leader named Suyitno. Suyitno was a dancer and singer for a *Kethoprak* (Javanese folk theater) group. His family celebrated with the whole village, presenting many performances and enjoying festive food for the special occasion. His daughter and many other family members performed certain dances: *Tanduk Majeng* (a dance from the nearby island of Madura), "Gendjer-Gendjer" (the previously mentioned song and dance from the Banyuwangi region), and *Adon Adon Sumping.* These dances are mostly new creations based on traditional Javanese dance styles. Culturally Madurese (from the island of Madura) or Osing (an ethnic group from the Banyuwangi region of East Java), they are performed together with gamelan music played in the *Slendro* scale. That evening, accompanied by other family members and villagers, Suyitno's daughter also sang a song

entitled "Berdikari" (meaning "standing on your own feet"), which had been promoted by the first president, Sukarno. Not long after the celebration, Suyitno, the new village leader, was suddenly arrested by the military and taken to an unknown place.[34]

Pak Suyitno was never returned to his family. After his arrest, his daughter and the dancers and other performers from that night, including those who had only helped prepare the food and other festivities, were all questioned by the Army; because such activities are usually delegated to women, those questioned were mostly female. On the day of the interrogations, many other villagers came home to find family members missing and were given no explanation for their disappearance. Several of those who were not taken—particularly those villagers who had attended the celebration—had their identity cards recalled by a government officer. The only explanation they were given was that they had been reported as PKI members, and they henceforth would lose the right to vote.

After the event, none of the participants, or the interviewees, ever danced or performed publicly again. Instead, every week, for more than thirty years, they reported to the local district military office *(Korem)*. The many forms of repression, including the economically and socially deadly practice of stamping the identity cards (KTP) of the New Order's former prisoners with "ET" for *ekstapol* or ex–political prisoner (if they even were issued a KTP), continued up until the very end of Suharto's presidency. The stamp thus ensured a "life sentence," even for those released after ten or fifteen years.[35] In this context, despite the state's somewhat arbitrary system for classifying those associated with the Communist Party as more or less dangerous, in the everyday context of society, there was generally little sense of different degrees of guilt or involvement; everyone involved was often considered equally culpable, no matter how minor their participation or tenuous their link to the party.

It may be due to fear of indiscriminate retribution that many survivors and witnesses to the events of the massacres still remain mute, both nationally and internationally, leaving the reproduction and distribution of knowledge about the events to the totalizing mechanism of the New Order regime. Like the scores of vanished spouses, parents, and relatives, then, huge numbers of villagers' dances and songs for community and family gatherings vanished, just as the corporeal memories of their movements and sounds were muted through the enforcement of new laws, carried out nationwide by officials and fearful or vigilant civilians alike. Yet a few dance forms from villages such as that of *Pak* Suyitno were kept, having been deemed a valuable national heritage by the state, and were later performed in different settings, such as the celebration of Independence Day and other official commemorative holidays.

Because such practices were in effect taken apart and "cleaned," reconstructed, and given to new, state-aligned bodies to practice before they were paraded out for state functions, however, the dancers who once performed in the village remained unwanted. As "subalterns," many of them still do not yet feel safe to speak out because every year, while certain things change, state policy on national history and performing arts remains unbendingly the same. For these women, and for other dancers and former students in the national education system such as myself, the passing of national time, following the flow of years, might be said to run backward even as it races toward the future, returning each year to the same point that officially marks the "birth of the nation" under Suharto. This point serves as the anchor for a way of seeing and remembering—the national perspective—and for the policies and cultural "unity" that continually guide our behavior and expression.

Each year we are all collectively pulled back to that time— October 1, 1965, the zero hour—through the medium of cinema, with eyes on the screen, and memories set to "record" for the obligatory school report the following day. We are forcibly reminded of the acts of those who are said to have threatened the entire nation, of the communists and the violent, dancing "wild women" of Gerwani. We are reminded of the unalterable importance of these acts, of Suharto's response, and of our duty as citizens to keep this history, and the perspective that allows us to visualize it, deeply embedded within ourselves. We, like the nation as defined by the state, must in some senses never change, learn, or grow, but rather we always return to the same point, that of "our" birth, the zero hour.

In some ways, then, we are not simply an "amnesia" project, because every child is forced to remember the narrative that the state has reconstructed: all of us Indonesian children must *remember,* and we are forbidden to forget. This is also a "remembering" project, then, based on national memories that have reconstructed the identities of all those who were left standing after the bloody rise of the state, telling us who is illicit and who is hero. In the words of Benedict Anderson, from "remorselessly accumulating cemeteries . . . the nation's biography snatches . . . exemplary suicides, poignant martyrdoms, assassinations, executions, wars, and holocausts. But, to serve the narrative purpose, these violent deaths must be remembered/forgotten as 'our own.'"[36] In Indonesia, we know we remember the dancer on screen, who always appears precisely on cue surrounded by violence and murder; and we know we must *not* remember, or speak of, the other things that we remember, and thus we carry them on in "silence," and yet our controlled movements are ever so slightly swayed by their weight within our bodies.

3. HISTORICIZING VIOLENCE

Memory and the Transmission of the Aesthetic

In *Where Memory Dwells,* Macarena Gómez-Barris suggests that those most affected by the legacies of dictatorship continue to live with the presence of violence in their bodies, in their daily lives, and in the identities they pass down to younger generations.[1] Like Gómez-Barris, in my own work such memories of violence contain the potential to become seeds of resistance and counter-memorialization. However, unlike Chile under Pinochet in *Where Memory Dwells,* with its active, critical documentation by exile communities and internal dissidents, my analysis of Indonesia reveals a halting and indirect actualization of embodied memory over the course of several decades. In my own experience, and that of other dancers in East Java, this was enacted not by filmmaking or overtly political artwork, but rather through strong family leadership—women's covert transmission of artistic practice to their children—that implanted fragments of unrestrained "memory" in the minds and movements of many young dancers.

In this chapter I examine how the strategic transmission of dance technique in the context of villages and family compounds can effect a coded distribution of different types of narratives concerning history, power, and state order, narratives aimed at an eventual *coming to fruition* in the form of resistive practice. Historically, in the case of Indonesia, the visibility and effectiveness of such approaches has been hindered by the ubiquitous, embedded fear of the threat of real punishment associated with the "misuse" of the dancing body. However, the government's heightened sense of concern also suggests its tacit acknowledgment of the dancing body's symbolic power as a weapon, the wielding of which has, throughout history, been dependent on the ability of those in power to find, "develop," and control a variety of talented dancers, choreographers, and master teachers.

Using memory and the analysis of technique as a methodological approach to search for such alternate narrations or "resistive" knowledge within the body, I return to the scenes of my own childhood, through which I seek access to an "invisible" and contested crossroads of influence and narration. At that time, after the widespread killings of artists had for the most part ceased, the state fought for continuing control through the presence—in many different guises—of its agents, offering various levels of recognition and mobility to those who were deemed *handal,* here signifying a combination of polished skill and unflagging commitment (reliability) to a group or organization. In this context, I interrogate the attempts of the New Order state to crush the local influence—and resulting unpredictability and particularity of meaning—of certain practices through the process of preservation and replication, a globalized technique that has continued, essentially unchanged, in the post-Suharto era of *Reformasi.*

For my analysis of the relevance of rural tradition in Indonesia and its absorption into broader discourses after 1965, I take the method of Assia Djebar in *Fantasia: An Algerian Cavalcade* as an important point of departure.[2] In her intellectually daring and hybrid historical "novel," Djebar reimagines future knowledge as a transmission of resistance, enabled by the (nonetheless questionable and fraught) use of colonial language in order to return to the memories of childhood, reliving—and re*thinking* and interpreting—moments of encounter from the perspective of the present. In this context, I employ my current understanding of the Indonesian state's official "language" of technique in order to reanalyze the continuing movement and reconfiguration of dance practice that began three years prior to my own birth. In so doing, I seek to question the unspoken meanings and assumptions of inclusion and difference, na-

tional tradition and alterity—the result of an understanding of officialized technique as signifying precisely which bodies are appropriate, valid, or "safe."

These collective meanings, both crystal clear and impossible to
fully understand, are what accompany gesturing, dancing bodies from
village-level competitions to regional performances, potentially offering future access to travel and the crossing of international borders.
Like Djebar, however, as I look back, I no longer seek the fixity of
meaning that promises mobility. Rather, I look for the ways in which
other, equally slippery "facts" and impressions may have lodged
themselves in our bodies through the repetition of movements, the
details, inflections, and specific connotations of which might continue to live, submerged and smuggled within the imposed broader
language of nationalized form, of patriotism and travel.

I begin, then, with one of the ends of my training as a dancer:
travel and performance on the international stage. I take such much-
coveted endings, however, as a point of departure for a critical exploration of their historical origins—the complex, transnational series
of occurrences that serve as their conditions of possibility. In light
of this analysis, I examine the ways in which the imposed, co-opted
goal of national and global performance, despite the unceasing efforts of the state, may precisely serve as a touchstone to examine the
past, thus opening the potential for a future state of affairs that no
one—authoritarian government, "unruly" or state-aligned dancer, or
transnational political-artistic confederation—can reliably predict
or control.

Jejer the Forbidden Dance

*It is August 1994, she travels to Saigon (Ho Chi Minh City). She
performs at an event celebrating both Vietnam's introduction into
ASEAN (Association of South East Asian Nations) and Indonesia's Independence Day. Everyone in the dance group is a civil
servant as well as a performer, carrying passports and a full roster of
documents along with luggage stuffed with official traditional dance
costumes. They are all dressed in uniform, their matching blue batik
jackets representing their nation. Most of the group members are*

female, since women perform a majority of the dances on cultural missions. She herself had been chosen to perform Jejer, but she was surprised and puzzled by the state's decision to include this particular dance. Jejer is not a Javanese court dance. Unlike Srimpi or Bedhaya, it has not been promoted abroad as part of the government's agenda since Dutch colonial times. Rather, as an official Indonesian folk dance, Jejer was derived from a longer performance called Gandrung, performed by females during the village harvest celebration. As such, on stage it does not employ a graceful manner or display an abstract philosophical approach to the body. Rather, in this form, the body moves rapidly, with circular torso movements, lively darting of the eyes, and extended arms as the hands reach high in a fanlike motion. This cultural mission to Vietnam would be the first mission to include a performance of Jejer, and it was through this travel—because of a cultural mission abroad—that she learned why the dance was included in the cultural mission that year.

These are my travel notes from a state cultural mission to Vietnam in 1994. The dance troupe, which consisted of Indonesian state and civil servant dancers, performed both court dance and folk dances that had already passed through the state processes of nationalization and standardization. As such, their movements and costumes were carefully aligned with government ideals of "purity" of form and content, which in the national context are disseminated and enforced down to the village level. *Jejer,* which was banned following the massacres of 1965–66, by the mid-1990s had "returned" and been inducted into the national dance curriculum. Taught in the *Tari Daerah Lain* (Dance of Other Regions—meaning basically everything outside of the Central Javanese Court) program as a folk dance of East Java, *Jejer* can be used to fulfill an elective requirement for dance undergraduates in the Yogyakarta Arts Institute. Since its reinstatement by the government, *Jejer* has once again become a major form, now used to represent East Java in national dance competitions where regional troupes compete for top honors (and cash) in the capital city, Jakarta. My surprise at its inclusion in the cultural mission to Vietnam was thus mediated by my own memories of the power of rurally based forms to entertain and bring together enthusiastic crowds at the local level. But I knew that the road bridging suspicion, censure, and elimination or arrest of practitioners and the stage in Vietnam was rough and full of potentially fatal twists and turns.

Kasar: Redeveloping Rural Economies of Dance

After the mid-1960s, the construction of an ever-widening gap separating and differentiating court and non-court culture was emphasized through the reintroduction of specific, traditional social values, such as *adiluhung* (refined, elegant, and historically rooted in the principles of the aristocracy) and the redefinition of familiar aesthetic measurements such as *halus*, or refined, and *kasar*, or rough and unrefined.[3] However, certain forms, practiced mostly in rural areas and villages and officially included in the division of *halus* and *kasar*, can in some ways be located outside of this dichotomy altogether. These dances are called *Tari Kerakyatan*, or "folk dances," and their performance generally does not require the special contexts or staging of the aforementioned cultural events. Dances such as *Reyog*, *Jathilan*, *Topeng*, *Hadrah*, and *Tayub*—all forms that originated outside the palace—were reintroduced by the New Order as *kasar*, or "unrefined." Yet in the forms' own cultural contexts, the value of refined and unrefined often relates to a completely different scale, based on specific village codes. For example, in *Jathilan*, the success of the performance, that which defines it as distinguished or well developed, is traditionally judged by how many of the dancers enter into a trance state, as indicated by their movements appearing to become completely *out* of control. In this sense, the value of the technique as rough—and the fact that it is achieved through a trance state in which the dancer is purportedly no longer consciously controlling his or her movements—may exceed the state's conceptualization of *kasar* as related to, or striving for, the refined, *halus* gestures of palace dance.

Mainly for this reason, while promoting *Jathilan* as a traditional art form, the New Order instituted a ban on the practice of "real" trance in most performances, as the form was increasingly used to entertain tourists, or, on occasion, even visiting dignitaries, to whom representations of Indonesia's rural diversity were increasingly shown

Jathilan: a public performance for the inauguration or certification of a village troupe in Central Java after undergoing *pembinaan* (official "guidance" in proper dance form and exhibition) from the Institute of the Arts (ISI), Yogyakarta. "Turonngo," Sentolo, Wates, Central Java. Photographer/copyright: Rachmi Diyah Larasati, 2012.

as a kind of sidebar to the palace arts. According to many sources, however, the wild, often death-defying feats of trance continued to occur at certain times in more remote areas, where alternate economies of movement were more difficult to eradicate (they were useful to local officials in various ways) and were "switched back on" whenever possible. Thus *Jathilan* performances in many instances continued to be measured through community belief in supernatural powers, which circulated through a localized shamanistic hierarchy that excluded the purview of the palace and conferred status upon the village.[4]

Instead of a stage or court pavilion, these dances are mostly performed on empty land such as a rice field that has been dried during a harvest transition, the yard of the village headman, or a vacant sugar plantation. The audiences for such performances are mostly children and male adults from the surrounding area, although on some occasions the crowds are predominantly male and female youth. In recent years, these performances have become a popular setting for both young villagers and outsiders alike to "hang out" *(nongkrong),* although the settings are still considered by many to be "low class" or "cheap" and are therefore not attractive to many of the more cosmopolitan oriented youth of Indonesia. The shows themselves combine dance, acrobatics, and highly specialized skills incorporating fire, eating glass, or stepping on burning coals or sharp objects, which require strict training and preparation. The musical accompaniment is provided by a much smaller gamelan orchestra than that which is used for court dance, and the movements themselves often imitate those of soldiers and animals.

Other dances, such as *Tayub* or *Ronggeng,* have also been very popular among villagers; they traditionally operated in terms of specific, local systems of value, which often sought to capitalize on their distance from the refined culture of the palace. (In academic writing, these dance forms are described as "ritual practice," performed during and prior to the harvest ceremony.)[5] Because they allow female dancers and male audience members to dance together in the village context, they are considered low class and unrefined. Yet their popularity and ability to draw large, mostly male crowds to various types of events, including political rallies, resulted in a disproportionate amount of scrutiny during and after the rise of the New Order. Reflected in my own experiences as a young dancer and enthusiastic spectator, the performance of *Tayub* and *Ronggeng* was a revelatory site of enjoyment mixed with tense contestation, in which the conditions for local artists' power were visibly at odds with the state's dominant system of aesthetic value.

Pariyah: The Dialectic of Talent and Desire

Pariyah was her name, a childhood friend of mine. I never knew where her father was. She was five years older than me. What I knew about her was that she possessed the ability to sing and dance so profoundly that everyone in the village was stunned and adored her. So, when the school did not want to accept her because she was too poor and couldn't provide a letter from the military district stating she had no connection to her family's "unclean environment," she started to focus on learning Tayuban. *Because of her unusual level of skill, in the context of the village, she became something of a "star." The village head, police, military district officers, teachers, puppet master, and farmers were all eager members of her audience. Although the men were seated differently based on their class, on the field, waiting in line for a chance to dance with her, they gulped down Bintang beer with a unified sense of anticipation. In their left hands they prepared the money, excitedly looking forward to the opportunity to stuff it in her semi-exposed cleavage. Wasted from drink by the end of the show, they seemed to have forgotten Pariyah's lack of a clean environment letter or that she lived alone without the father who had first taught her to follow the music of those performances.*

Pariyah became the star of a red village, and when she was still very young she owned her own house and an old Dokar, *or horse carriage. She was a female dancer and singer that the villagers were both envious and proud of because many of them were also unable to send their daughters to school, but they lacked the talent to sing or dance like Pariyah. Although the "red" is a burden because it marks your genealogy, trapping you in the embodiment of the worst possible identity, stopping your steps like a machine that can be turned on and off at the will of others, it was different for Pariyah. Through her "unrefined" corporeality, Pariyah was able to reflect, in a code readable by those who wished to understand and analyze the experience of recent history, the intersection of culture and state violence. Many Islamic conservatives dismiss the presence of those young women like Pariyah by categorizing their performances as a mere resource for male desire, made more sinful, according to the Qur'an, by the consumption of alcoholic beverages that frequently accompanies such events. But by inviting the man from* Koramil *(the military district officer) to be the first to dance with her and the police officers to be next, Pariyah ensured the event would receive the proper permits. Unlike the conditions that to some extent enabled the state's actions in 1965, in this performance site, the normally*

*strong collaboration between Islamic conservatism and military power
was broken, and for once they disagreed on the appropriate response
to the female dancing body.*

*Post 1965, with Communist Party members no longer in the
audience, the code of conduct, rules, and training that govern the
performance of* Tayub *were also changed. Tumi, Pariyah's mother,
mentioned that she preferred the ex-Nationalist Party members and
military officers now making up her daughter's audience, because
they provided better protection than did the old comrades of the
PKI. Her connections to them enabled her to escape prison when it
was discovered her husband had been a member of BTI (Barisan
Tani Indonesia), a farmers' association accused of being a branch
of the PKI (personal interview, 2002). Tumi and Pariyah, who are
illiterate, seemed unconcerned with the news reports about the government's new morality guidelines aimed at family dance practices
like theirs. Tumi never bothered to pay attention to my rehearsals
with the new official cultural representative, who, like his colleagues
all over Indonesia, came to our village and trained young, aspiring
dancers to move in a more "refined" way. Yet she would enthusiastically discuss my eye and hip movements when I secretly rehearsed
the* Gandrung *(a village dance for harvest ceremonies, containing
a section in which men dance together with female dancers, but not
involving alcohol or money exchange) with my grandmother in back
of my house. Unlike* Tayub, Gandrung *was completely banned
(instead of simply being restricted) in many red villages after 1965.
Yet as I rehearsed the movements, Tumi's eyes were riveted on me
just as when she saw Pariyah on the field singing the* Tembang
(song for Tayub). *She said both forms,* Tayub *and* Gandrung,
*were popular and reached thousands of people in the villages before
the time of those murders.*

For Tumi, Pariyah's *Tayub* performance and my *Gandrung* performance, if compared to *Bondan* (a type of court dance), had a different corporeal significance. *Tayub* and *Gandrung,* which are inseparable from villagers' lives, engage Tumi's own corporeal memory and
its intimate, detailed, and very real ties to the more collective, local
experience of history. As Pariyah and I understood it, this corporeal

A young girl in East Java learns the Bondan form. (The dancer is not referred to in the text.) Dancer: Erlina Pantja Sulistjaningtyas, Malang, East Java, 1975. Photographer: Niecke Rochiatini. Copyright: Erlina Pantja Sulistjaningtyas.

memory was linked to the communication of tradition in the village, a kind of moving, living concept containing meanings that we were old enough to carry but perhaps too young to completely grasp. Yet, in spite of the fact that *Tayub* and *Gandrung* were transmitted through generations of revered dancers in Tumi's region, on a national scale, many of those who practiced the forms were severely marginalized by the New Order. As a result, many *Tayub* and *Gandrung* groups were required to undergo *pembinaan,* or "guidance," from artists who belonged to the centralized cultural establishment and whose primary training and background was in court dance. Ultimately, most forms from outside the palace began to visibly conform to the movements of the Javanese courts, yet they were still considered unrefined and of lower artistic quality.

In many villages and towns of East Java, district heads invited dance instructors from the Yogyakarta palace to teach their children Javanese dances such as *Bondan, Srimpi, Kelono Topeng,* and *Bambangan Cakil* (an appended version of the *Mahabarata*). Festivals and dance competitions specifically showcasing the Javanese court dance genre occur almost every year all over Indonesia. Exceptional performance at these festivals offers the reward of a scholarship for further study at advanced institutions. Thus the state's practice of *pembinaan* and promotion of the value of *halus,* refined movement fosters standardization and a nationalized sense of tradition among villagers. Because such training can provide legitimization and the opportunity to perform nationally, it offers artists the opportunity to continue their family practice of dance as a part of officially sanctioned village cultural activities. Still, the various backgrounds and experiences of the officers sent to oversee the rural cultural activities affect the decisions that they make; many of them are dance or arts practitioners or former practitioners, and this training and cultural knowledge, some of which may not have come so directly from the state, is inevitably carried with them and may sway their opinions or decisions.

The Transmission of Technique: Grandmother's Yard

In my grandmother's yard, the women gathered, mostly wives and mothers who had just finished their routine weekly assembly called PKK or *Pendidikan Kesejahteraan Keluarga,* loosely translatable as "Women's Education on the Issues of Family Life." Such meetings are exclusively for women and are led by those whose status is based on their husbands' positions in the state-imposed hierarchy of village life. During the meetings attended by my grandmother's neighbors, the wife of the village headman, as a consultant and leader of the committee board for PKK, oversaw the process of implementation of her husbands' list of tasks for regulating the "emancipation" of the women in the village, thus maintaining civil order in the areas targeted by the state for regulation, ranging from health issues (such as birth control and breast feeding) to approving traditional dress for Islamic wedding ceremonies. Training in the local dissemination of state policy (for example, regarding elections), environmental awareness, and state-approved dance practices was also often included.[6]

Yet in *this* circle, in my grandmother's yard, the talk was different. Whispering and mingling without regard to official status, addressing other members and neighbors informally, the women spoke at their own speed, and with their own language and topics, disregarding the orders and memories instilled by the official atmosphere of the PKK. The women here were mostly non–civil servants, yet they, too, were discussing the official commemoration and celebration of Independence Day that would soon be held in the village. Like the deliberations at the PKK meeting, they were debating the selection of a dance form for the event. Yet among the circle of women in the yard, the main focus of the forceful, whispered discussion was on the issue of who was going to perform; it seems the main candidate brought up in the formal meeting at the village office was not agreed on by all members. Normally, while they spoke, the women would glance toward the children practicing nearby, turning, dancing, and stepping. But this time, the focus was divided solely between their hushed words and the task of preparing a special *kenduri,* or offering, for the late Ngatini, a dancer who had recently gone missing and never returned.

In the corner of the yard, a young girl, Poniti, the daughter of the late Ngatini, had been learning how to move her hips and eyes differently from the way she was taught by her mother. A state official suggested the new movements were better because they were "not too seductive." Yet the girl, who also practiced under the supervision of my grandmother, seems more attentive to the discussion of the worrisome news of her sibling's rejection from a job at the local school office as a guard. Her relatives all blame the misfortune on her mother's disappearance; a missing family member is read as a sure

Tari Topeng, an East Javanese form frequently taught in schools and used in regional competitions broadcast on state television. (The dancer is not referred to in the text.) Dancer: Erlina Pantja Sulistjaningtyas, Surabaya, East Java, 1978. Photographer: Niecke Rochiatini. Copyright: Erlina Pantja Sulistjaningtyas.

sign of punishment by the state, a contagious curse whose ill effects flow onward via the branches of the victim's family tree.

While Poniti will be a part of the official village dance troupe, the legacy of her mother's knowledge and skill that has already been transmitted and spread through our community will both "disappear" and continue to exist in the daughter's body. The official never acknowledged her mother's disappearance as such, yet her missing body and the knowledge it represented are tacitly recognized as containing the potential to powerfully renegotiate the suppression of memory. Therefore, the daughter and former students of the "mysteriously" disappeared dancer are watched closely and handled with great suspicion by the myriad agents of the state and those under their influence.

For several weeks preceding the Independence Day celebration, the dance practice in my grandmother's yard had been undergoing a restructuring process according to new guidelines from the head of the village, based on the comments of the regional arts council. Poniti and the other dancers rehearsed extensively because of the changing of certain gestures. During the celebration of Independence Day, we were to perform at the home of the regent, as part of a competition with other nearby village troupes. The winners would be included in the national dance team and their photographs added to an official tourism brochure.

On such occasions, then, the regional mapping of cultural inheritance mediates local participation in performance that is marked ultimately to extend far beyond regional borders, potentially entering the international stage (which, in the case of nonpalace performance, includes the "stages" attended locally by international tourists and officials) as a representation of Indonesian national culture. As the dancing body travels and reproduces itself through the images captured by visitors and tourists, the local negotiation of cultural practice is connected to international space and foreign capital. The participation, or aspiration to participate, in this system by young dancers is often taken for granted as an ultimate goal—one that strives for glory in the fulfillment of obligation or duty on a national scale—and is structured as such according to state mandate.

As the daughter of the late Ngatini, Poniti performed the same dance for which her mother was previously known as a master performer and teacher. Yet in the sociopolitical context of the early New Order era, her movements were both "real" and simulacra, constructing an image with a certain resemblance to her disappeared mother, reoccupying the dancing space from which her mother was forcibly removed but without an outwardly obvious attempt to acknowledge the fate of Ngatini or the mass violence of the recent past. Further, through her mastery of movements and technique, Poniti will be inducted into the militaristic space in which the function of her dance reaches far beyond the village and its feminine shamanistic rituals, where the eroticism of folk dance enters the purview of a national event in subdued and modified form. As M. Jacqui Alexander proposes in "The Erotic Autonomy as a Politics of Decolonialization," "sex and gender lie, for the state, at the juncture of the disciplining of the body and the control of the population and are, therefore, constitutive of those very practices." In this context, then, an analysis of the state's structuring "patriarchal imperatives" may enable a further examination and decoding of the ways in which "gestures of normalization exert and deploy force, generate new sexual meanings . . . and punish women in disproportionate ways for a range of imputed infractions."[7]

Magang: Collection, Consumption, and Transmission

In the corner of my grandmother's yard, a female civil servant who had been visiting the village to learn the local dance forms, kept writing and taking pictures. At the time, many of the local dances were being promoted as a valuable traditional heritage by the district office of cultural affairs. In between taking notes, the civil servant occasionally imitates the dance as she observes, and every evening she studies through magang *(a structured transmission of form with a master practitioner who is positioned outside of official arts institutions) with another teacher in the village.*

Along with pembinaan, *as I would learn,* magang *was the second, and perhaps more insidious, method of expression of the interest of the state and the national arts institute in rural, or "folk" forms. Both seemingly involve a sense of intimacy through the learning and*

*transfer of movements and active bodily experience. Yet the geopolitics
of the body and the historiography of learning dance are reconstructed,
in this case producing a new content and value in the performance of
Gandrung, while clearly marking the state's involvement (at least
here, where its agents had identified themselves and were taking
notes) in the embodiment and understanding of specific practices as
forms that are both "traditional" and "inherited."*

Like the civil servant who came to my grandmother's yard to
observe our training, in searching my memories—and the movements that I can still call forth from my body—I *look out* for the
presence of particular details, those laden with something that feels
particularly *of* my grandmother and the experience of my training
and socialization within the walls of her house. Yet my aim is to
highlight and crystallize these details in my writing as intervention,
while our "honored guest" was intent on taking them *down,* examining and acknowledging their presence in order to map, subsume,
and suppress.

In this sense, the presence of outsiders in the family compound
in relation to its function as a space for dance was not a new phenomenon. During the colonial time, many foreign officers were sent
to spaces of learning and performance like my grandmother's home,
with orders to document in detail every single step of every dance
form practiced there. This archiving of life, of dancing bodies into
materiality, pieces of history, is clearly a site of dispersion and multiple translations, mediated through the gaze of the witness. As a
process of interpretation, it often produced new names, recategoriza-
tions, and, indeed, specific reformulations of the cultural identity of
the colonized according to the wants or needs of the colonizer.

One example of this process of observation, exposure, and change
is the use of white socks (without shoes) for female *Gandrung* dancers,
beginning in 1930, as per the aesthetic guidance of a Dutch colonial
officer.[8] Dutch "development" or "civilization" of Indonesian arts
continued to occur until independence, leaving a map of specific
aesthetic marks of embodied colonial influence on the traditional
movements of female practitioners of *Gandrung* and other forms.
Like the New Order state, which came to power only fifteen years

after the Dutch were officially banished, the former colonizers' attention was heavily focused on the aesthetic value of women. Thus, although prior to 1965 men also performed *Gandrung,* only the female dancers were made to cover their bare feet with the European stockings. Dutch influence also shows itself in the specific categorization of dance practices like *Gandrung,* which at that time were also viewed as clearly distinct from, and inferior to, the refined aesthetic value attached to court or palace practice. Thus, in the modern era of Indonesia's independence, the label of "folk dance," now called *tari rakyat,* has retained its status as an extremely important—and loaded—signifier of the massive status gap between village and palace performers.

In the contemporary context, the act of documentation and standardized development of various dances continues, with the colonial ethnographic moment replaced by that of the local civil servant (who is, at various levels, still considered foreign in most village contexts). The presence of such agents in the process of *magang* and *pembinaan* informs the systematic encounter with the (re)interpretation and (re)presentation of the dancing body as centralized cultural policy. In addition to the process of learning and documentation in *magang,* *pembinaan* involves the presence of other state-aligned outsiders who arrive in teams of evaluators and "trainers" aimed at (re)imbuing villages with the forms that have previously been extracted and reconstructed according to the perceived needs of the central government. Thus, the young girls who study dance in villages are exposed to the ideology of culture as an instrument of the state, and also necessarily to the system of desire that posits the distant reward of scholarships and potential mobility for which all—even the majority who are not selected as *handal* or "talented or committed enough"— must internalize government doctrine in order to become eligible.

Thus, the production of narrative and history for each dance that is disseminated to hopeful candidates and later embodied and reproduced in performance by students and professors is aligned with the sanitized and recategorized information approved by the state for public distribution. The story of the late Ngatini and many other former *Gandrung* dancers is of course not permitted to enter into classroom discussions or to be recorded or distributed in any written form, including the ethnographic studies with their detailed "histories" of the dances. Yet as in the case of colonial strategies of knowledge gathering, categorization, and control, memory and artistic practice have proved their resilience, and the power of dance as a tool for expression has often shown itself to be based, at least in part, on the very complexity and slipperiness of meaning, context, and notions of aesthetic value. In this spirit, I attempt a thorough analysis of the intricate and erratic historical path of a particular rurally based form, from its banning and reappropriation as a state-aligned but peripheral element of Indonesian "diversity" to its later, surprising (given its historical political connotations) reemergence on the national and international stage.

The Return of *Jejer:* Complex History Reclaimed

The dance form *Jejer* (which I described performing in Vietnam earlier in the chapter) was for the state seen as perhaps the most "subversive" variant of the form *Gandrung,* the structure and movements of which are also quite similar to the controversial *Tayub* discussed previously. *Jejer* serves here as an example of how the state has attempted to take an established set of movements and, over time, put it through a process of resignification so that the meanings it encodes are historically altered and politically realigned. From the perspective of the present, my own fortuitous convergences with the form, enabled in part by the "folk" techniques I acquired in my grandmother's yard, thus provide an additional analytical tool: the excavation and reexamination of memories and corporeal experience that officially belong, along with the rest of my knowledge and skills as a dancer, to the Ministry of Education, the Indonesian state.[9]

To begin with, during and shortly after the 1965–66 massacres, *Jejer* came to signify marginal practice and forbidden behaviors; later, as it "changed hands"—and bodies—it was construed as standing for the valued diversity of Indonesia and its upward trajectory in the international sphere of cultural exchange and development. The concept of "development" in Indonesian cultural policy depends on an ongoing process of appropriating and nationalizing the arts as specific cultural activities shared by all Indonesians; that is, as part of the nation-state's collective cultural identity, itself a construct intended to promote national stability. Here, *national stability* is a term that refers to the state's assessment of its own security; stability, in other words, means the successful prevention of any potential disruption to state authority.

In previous chapters, I included an analysis of the infrastructure of state control over culture. One of the examples of this system is the Ministry of Culture, operating from the center (Jakarta as a center of government), to the periphery (regional, local villages) as a superstructure for the mechanisms of control acting on Indonesian cultural practices. Although different mechanisms of control operate within the public cultural sphere, including the institutionalized cultural practices of the educational system, both mechanisms are based on center–periphery models of cultural policy. In the public cultural sphere (the realm of nonacademic, institutionalized arts practice), control is maintained by the Ministry of the Interior and the Ministry of Culture and Tourism, with regional management handled by a department of arts in each area. In the academic sphere, control is maintained by the Ministry of Education in cooperation with the Ministry of Culture and Tourism, including the Directorate General of Education and/or the Directorate General of Culture.

The level of authority given to the Ministry of Culture and Tourism (both during the New Order and currently) as a control system for both academic and nonacademic cultural activities demonstrates how urgent the Indonesian state considers cultural policy. The promotion of national stability, as well as the concept of "cultural practice" as a part of a nationalist agenda and as a measure of a citizen's loyalty, is mandatory. One effect of this systematization and nationalization of form is the standardization of certain dance movements such that they are explainable in terms of specific established symbols, meanings, and myths. Another is the regulation of eligibility governing the selective inclusion of particular dance forms as part of the nation's official culture (such as "refined" court forms or refashioned "folk" forms) and the exclusion of others (such as regional dances by marginal cultural groups).

The Beginning of the End: Osing Culture Vanished

Jejer is a dance from the region of East Java called Banyuwangi, which is dominated by Osing speakers but also contains pockets of ethnic Madurese, Chinese, and some Javanese. The Banyuwangi are famous among Indonesians for their devoted yet hybrid religious practice of Islam, combined with rich, local mysticism. Among other ethnic groups, the Banyuwangi region is known as a place where *santet* (black magic or spiritual power) is produced and "sent," usually for a fee, to inflict itself upon the lives of those designated by the sender. In fact, in 1997–98, when Suharto's regime was in its final days, there were mass killings in this area of certain *kyai* (Islamic clerics) or *dukun* (shamans) who had been labeled, by both common belief and state narrative, as *dukun santet,* or shamans practicing black magic. Although it is impossible to convict someone of such acts, in this case, rumor and gossip became powerful enough to serve as justification for their deaths. (This situation showed some disturbing similarities to the events of 1965, especially in the methods of killing utilized.) In addition to those suspected *dukun santet* who were murdered, hundreds more reportedly hanged themselves.

Like its infamous combination of religion and magic, the dance practiced in Banyuwangi, *Jejer,* places itself far outside of more generalized understandings of Muslim religious activity in Indonesia. To begin with, the dancers, all of whom are female, display their hair and upper torso, body parts forbidden to be shown in public by the Qur'an (as interpreted by more conservative local *ulama* or Islamic teachers). But beyond that, in 1965, *Jejer* was targeted by both the military (acting as the emerging state) and conservative Islam in their joint efforts to eradicate various kinds of "evil." Before 1965, *Jejer* was known as an informal, "proletarian" form, a lively and boisterous dance performed by villagers most evenings during harvest time, with no clear line drawn between audience and dancer. At these festivities, everyone could move freely, with men and women dancing together without deference to each other's religious or political identity. During the New Order's reconstruction of culture on a national scale, because of the political and economic dominance of Islamic clerics in the region, *Jejer* was cast as a "minority" practice in two important ways:

it was not "Islamic" enough to be protected under the power of the more conservative (and well-connected) local clerics, and its folk-based context—its practice by and for the *masyarakat pedesaan,* or village community, rather than local elites—created a vast gap between its practitioners and those of the Javanese court, another safe cultural zone during the killings and arrests in 1965. Moreover, because of its connection to the "proletarian" rural poor, practitioners of *Jejer* have become associated, whether justifiably or not, with certain cultural groups related to Lekra, the People's Cultural Association, whose members were targeted during and after 1965.[10]

In some cases this assumption was accurate; these were the only cultural institutions that concerned themselves with life at the village level prior to the rise of the New Order. During the Sukarno era, the state "culture manifesto" was broad enough to encompass the inclusion of minority groups within a common political struggle, and this historical connection with leftist ideals (although at the time it was considered far more mainstream) has also made *Jejer* and *Gandrung* (the longer form) groups the targets of anti-communist violence. The banning of the two forms, however, does not mean that the dances themselves contained or expressed "communist ideology"—in fact, some performances of *Jejer, Gandrung,* and other targeted practices were given by explicitly anti-communist members of the nationalist PNI party—but if a dance was performed or thought to have been performed by members of Lekra, Gerwani, or the PKI, then the form itself was most often considered "tainted" by association and automatically forbidden. In Bayuwangi, during the 1965–66 massacres, allegations of communist involvement from the Indonesian state were compounded by preexisting personal disputes among the local citizenry. At that time, the accusation of a rival's or enemy's connections to "communism" became a convenient way to get rid of them for good, creating an atmosphere of fear and suspicion in which the practitioners of the region's beloved traditional arts were singled out as "exemplary" scapegoats. The result was that artists were arrested en masse and many people simply vanished without a trace. Few folk performers in Banyuwangi survived, and those who did faced stigmatization, marginalization, and persecution until the fall of Suharto in 1998. In many cases—like the millions of other citizens victimized during the rise of Suharto—they continue to be targeted by neighbors, police, and other officials for whom New Order policies and social structures still form the basis of justifiable thought and action.[11]

Because of state policy, the categorization of individual artists as *terlibat,* or "involved" (with communist activity), or as contributing to an "unclean environment" had an immense impact on families, and often entire communities. As Leslie Dwyer states in her work "The Intimacy of Terror," "Post-1965 fragmented Balinese families were perversely knitted back together by the 'clean environment' *[bersih lingkungan]* policy of the New Order government, which claimed that spouses, parents, siblings, children and even grandchildren of those marked as communists were 'infected' by political 'uncleanliness' and thus were to be barred from participation in the government bureaucracy or civil society organizations."[12]

For performers of *Jejer* and *Gandrung* in East Java, then, families were perversely knitted into networks of secrecy and self-defense against further victimization, as outcasts and groups of *former* artists whose generations-old traditional practice—for many, their main source of income—was taken and never returned. Instead, it was effectively transformed into government "property." The state's actions thus functioned to reshape the landscape of performance and tradition in multiple areas, along with much of what had previously constituted the socioeconomic and legal structures, political alliances, and practice.

Privately, however, certain groups of banned practitioners in East Java engaged in an unofficial, "silent" resistance to the ban, secretly sustaining their practice of the music of *Jejer* and *Gandrung.*[13] This continuing practice, like the surreptitious activities within the walls and enclosed yards of *terlibat* dancers, can perhaps be seen as an indication of both the artistic, political passion and the socioeconomic desperation that stirred within the bodies of censured performers. At the regional level, despite the support necessarily shown by Banyuwangi's local leaders for the New Order and its centrally administered cultural policies, the removal of a major source of pride, income, and mobility was unlikely to be seen as an entirely positive outcome. Thus, only a few years after the rise of Suharto and the resulting disappearance of *Jejer,* the *Bupati* (region head) of Banyuwangi, working with a federal government representative, moved to reinstate many of the local Osing art forms considered polluted by association with the left, forms that had, in the past, put Banyuwangi "on the map."

In the process, female civil servants were of course sent to the region to learn the dance forms (*Jejer* in particular), and the state took over its teaching and practice, regulating it via several regional institutional bodies. This did not, however, change government policies toward the "subversive" practitioners who had originally performed and played the music (they were still treated as forbidden, leftist subversives), but it did begin to change attitudes toward the form itself.

A few years later, elements of *Gandrung*—primarily the textually based performances of traditional poetry and the musical form and instrumentation—began to be performed by "new" practitioners under the guidance of HASBI *(Himpunan Seni Budaya Islam),* an Islamic cultural institution supported by the military and interested in the practice and promotion of Indonesian art forms identified as Muslim. (Here we can see the conformity of local Islam to the nationalized model of cultural self-representation; in this case it works in favor of the reemergence of a banned form.) HASBI was formed in 1955 and was originally founded by the *Angkatan Darat* (Army ground forces), which later initiated KASBI (*Kesatuan Aksi Kesenian dan Budaya Indonesia*—the Organization for the Unification of Indonesian Arts and Culture). Not surprisingly, this new, state-approved administration of the forms imposed strict regulations as to where, when, and by whom they could be taught and performed and edited and modified the associated poetic texts. Under this new authority, *Gandrung* and *Jejer* were limited to regional competitions among groups of elementary and high school performers and excluded from national-level representations. (*Jejer* was considered the "mascot" form for Banyuwangi and thus was increasingly performed in interregional competition, although it was blocked from any more general representation as an "Indonesian" form.)

While the former *Jejer* and *Gandrung* artists kept up their secretive practices, it was perhaps a more "coincidental" series of occurrences that led to the reinstatement of *Jejer* on a national level. The subsequent return to relative prominence of the form could be seen in part as the paradoxical result of its continuing to officially exist while being performed only on rare, special occasions. The success of the New Order state apparatus in oversaturating various cultural markets with Javanese palace arts would also appear to be a key factor in the fortunes of the forbidden practice on the global stage.

Global Interest: Reclamation and State Protection

Throughout the 1990s, the Smithsonian Institute (and Smithsonian Folkways Recordings) carried out a massive archival project entitled *Music of Indonesia,* aimed at producing a comprehensive collection of recordings from many different parts of the archipelago. Excluded, however, was Javanese court music, which had been extensively witnessed, documented, and sold to fans of "world music" in Europe and the United States and is easily accessible to tourists who come to Indonesia. Recorded over the course of several years, the Smithsonian project resulted in an exhaustive collection containing more than twenty CDs marketed as part of the Smithsonian Folkways Records' World Music Series. For the researchers, anthropologists, and musicologists involved, the structure and sound of the music combined with singing in the local Osing language led to the classification of *Gandrung* (and with it, *Jejer*), following the state, as a "folk tradition." While there is no explicit mention in the promotional materials or liner notes of the forms' status as endangered or in need of preservation, there is nonetheless an implied sense of conflict between the traditional structures of music and dance—which are described, interestingly, as a method of keeping "order"—and various encroaching, social, religious, artistic, or economic or technological elements. Thus, despite lack of available, documented histories of *Gandrung* or *Jejer* and the resulting foray into "uncharted territory," the Smithsonian team clearly made an effort to find and record a sufficiently seasoned performer who could herself be seen as preserving the forms simply by continuing to dance and sing in the way in which she had previously been taught.

The fraught political history of the forms was perhaps unknown, and in any case left unaddressed, by the Smithsonian. Yet their quest to find, digitally record, and internationally distribute "one of the finest *living* singers [and dancers] of the music" (emphasis added) seems uncannily apt in light of the fact that the real danger to *Gandrung* and *Jejer* had come less from globalization or modernization than from state violence.[14] The Smithsonian's detailed, ethnographic approach may thus have been quite effective, albeit in largely unintended ways.

Certainly, the desire for the finest or "purest" existing practice of *Gandrung* would require a fairly extensive search for older practitioners, potentially putting in motion a process of questioning as to the current status or historical fates of known artists whose careers had been ended by the state. Further, the success of the *Music of Indonesia* recordings enabled a politically marked, suppressed form—officially limited to regional-level competitions run by branches of the state apparatus—to be accessed by a broad range of international audiences, many of whom were located in the West. The recordings were also promoted locally by MSPI (*Masyarakat Seni Pertunjukan Indonesia,* the Association of Indonesian Performing Arts), which garnered strong support from the Indonesian arts community. Because of this, in addition to international sales, the collection was purchased by many well-known local musicians, institutions, and schools, creating a larger public awareness and demand for *Gandrung* and its associated forms. In effect, then, the international mobility of the practice succeeded in influencing the rise of a stronger national interest in *Gandrung* and *Jejer.* This in turn gave the Indonesian state a new perspective on the artistic quality, and resulting political and economic marketability, of the forms. *Gandrung* and *Jejer* suddenly acquired a particularly seductive and desirable status, which appeared to hold the promise of potential alliances with other prestigious global projects similar to the Smithsonian series.

Historically, this is consistent with the political economy of folk arts in Indonesia (and almost certainly elsewhere) as a potential source of interest, able to draw appreciative gazes from outside a local (or occasionally national) constituency, producing aesthetic attraction and "political" sympathy for the lovely, unique, yet apparently threatened traditions, that is fairly easily converted into gains in influence and trade. After the international exposure offered by the Smithsonian's archiving and distribution of "endangered" (if they only knew) *Jejer* and *Gandrung* music—mirrored soon afterward by a national trend of increased interest in the forms—many arts institutes began offering *Jejer* to students, sponsoring extensive training for teachers, and in the process creating new "masters" of the practice.

Having myself, as a child, learned the longer and more detailed *Gandrung* form from my grandmother, and later completed the institutional requirements for mastery of *Jejer,* I became the first teacher of *Jejer* at a U.S. university. (I began instructing students in the form in 1998 during my residence at UCLA—the class I created was continued until 2003, when I was completing coursework for my doctorate.) However, since Javanese court dance had already been well established in many U.S. higher educational institutions, it was often suggested to me (by both U.S. and Indonesian educators) that *Jejer* was not refined enough as a cultural expression to be taught or performed outside of Indonesia; in short, it was "too local," and perhaps too "low," to travel and be appreciated globally in the academic dance context.

To my surprise, however, when I began teaching it in the United States, *Jejer* was quite popular with students, particularly the small group of Chinese Indonesians from Jakarta who signed up for the first course. I felt, in some ways, that bringing *Jejer* to California had been my own unique, "subversive" contribution to global arts discourse. Such sentiments were tempered by the fact, however, that during that time, my conception of the possibilities of a "resistive" practice was necessarily limited, and I did not explain to the students the version of the history of the form that I am detailing in this work. Instead, I contextualized the dance by using a typical ritual framework of village harvest and fertility. It is possible that these students in particular, many of whom had recently lived through the violent targeting of ethnic Chinese Indonesians in 1998—and whose parents may have been among the large percentage of Chinese victims in 1965—would have been open to a critical discussion of the history of *Jejer* and other Indonesian forms. However, during those years I myself was in the middle of a process of developing a broader, and more critical, understanding of the political situation in Indonesia and my own function within it as a traveling dance teacher and civil servant. Perhaps feeling the weight of my special blue passport, which marked my presence abroad as a cultural ambassador, for the time being, I decided to keep my "discoveries" about my job, and about the performance of my job, separate. At the very least, a public presentation challenging the view of culture put forth by the Indonesian government, and bolstered by much of the Western academic and arts establishment, might destroy the access I had gained to smaller, more critical subfields of dance, Asian studies, and anthropology in the United States. Such access had become a crucial source of my rapidly expanding perspective on the country of my birth, and so, for the moment, I remained publicly silent, although to a somewhat different end than that of my earlier performance of *Jejer* in Vietnam.

As a then-state dancer and representative, however, I perhaps must view my combination of tentative movements and frequent retreats to stillness as part of the truth of the function and pervasive influence of the state cultural apparatus: a mechanism that is, in important ways, itself determinant of the process of creation of this book, a work that nonetheless attempts to know more deeply, to identify, and to critique its own "source." In this context, a closer examination of *Jejer* and *Gandrung* points to the ways in which the politics of culture in Indonesia are tightly interwoven with the state's political agenda: after reclamation by the government, the forms, altered to signify culture as "safe" and innocuous, were practiced by state representatives, students, civil servants, members of HASBI, KASBI, and many other youths studying in state art schools. In both the case of the Smithsonian's "discovery" and the subsequent intensification of interest from the Indonesian state, the process of reclamation and appropriation has functioned through a "preservation"—accomplished by historical extraction and aesthetic reconstruction—of the forms' assumed original aesthetic and technical properties such that they take on the aura of classic, "timeless" artistry, whose value (while still at the level of folk) should be obvious to sophisticated, culturally aware audiences worldwide.

Conceived of as rescued by extraction from the forces of history and time, dance is narrowed down into form and technique, elements that appear easily duplicated and reprogrammed, through training, into nearly any body (or captured onto any visual or aural format).

Thus, form is imbued with meaning—connecting it to a depoliti-cized, generalized "past"—and "passed down" from state to official practitioner, and from practitioner to eager student. Questioning the given history or meaning of the dance would be unlikely in the context of a typical professor–student relationship and would al-most certainly limit the student's chances of advancing to the level of teacher and performer, and with it the possibility of mobility along the established local and global pathways of *Gandrung, Jejer,* and other officially approved dance forms. In the face of this ultimate end, of preservation and performance on the national or global stage, the violence and injustice perpetrated upon the *Gandrung* and *Jejer* dancer, labeled as an unruly body, subversive and in alliance with the left, become nearly impossible not to "forget."

Janger and *Jejer*: History and the Control of Intellectual Property

This process of amnesia production, of course, has not been limited to Javanese dances, or solely to *Jejer.* To illustrate the wider imple-mentation and impact of this process of first stigmatizing and then reclaiming popular dances, we briefly turn to the treatment of the Balinese form *Janger.* This dance is said to describe the joys of youth; in it, the dancers stand in two lines, the women in front and the men behind, performing the same movements and singing the same song. In the mid-1960s, two different groups in the same village would on occasion perform the dance simultaneously, with their division into "sides" based on the political party or institution with which the dancers in each group were affiliated. Generally, one of the dance troupes was aligned with the PNI, or Nationalist Party, and the other with Lekra. In 1965–66, there was strong competition between the two factions, each employing its own strategies to attract newcomers and amass a greater membership.[15] However, since both sides rep-resented large, well-established political and artistic organizations, there was no conception of such events as containing subversive ele-ments or the possibility of provoking real bloodshed.

Yet soon afterward, this commemoration of cultural and politi-cal affiliation became a means of justifying the selection of individuals for interrogation, imprisonment, or death, especially when the head of a cultural group was a Communist Party member or there was historical animosity between two groups with differing political alliances. On the local level, anti-left sentiment became a way to eliminate rival groups by categorizing others as communists. Using these tactics, members of the PNI or Nationalist Party were able to establish and maintain their cultural domination in many areas. The real—and often political—differences, however, were minimal: in both Lekra and PNI-affiliated groups, dances were practiced using the same music and staging techniques, and the movements used by both sides were the same as those employed currently in *Janger* as an official Balinese cultural repertoire. Yet despite the fact that *Janger* was still permitted, and even celebrated, when performed by non–Lekra groups after 1965, performers associated with Lekra were targeted and stigmatized for allegedly having practiced a "communist" art form. Today, *Janger* is often performed and toured abroad to promote the richness and sacred beauty of Balinese ritual dance.

Janger, then, faced a similar repositioning by the state as *Jejer.* What distinguishes the two cases is the absence of reappropriation in the performance of *Janger,* because the PNI group, aligned with official state policy, practiced the same form as those dancers in Lekra who were deemed opponents of the state. In this process of representation, new bodies were not needed to perform the dance because the PNI groups already had cultural access to mastery of the practice. Thus, the focus in this case was on completely erasing the "unclean bodies" through murder or imprisonment. The new form and function of *Janger* severs the practice from its historical connection to Lekra-aligned bodies, attaching it to a "clean" genealogy, free of communists, or, like *Jejer,* any openly acknowledged political implications whatsoever.

As this suggests, the capacity for building alliances with state policy is clearly very important in determining access and permission to practice *Janger,* based on the goal of keeping it "clean." Such political cleanliness is directly linked to the state's approval, promotion, and financial support of the form as signifier, producing a stable, idealized image, in this case of Bali as a representation of Indonesia's cultural diversity; as such, *Janger* has been fixed and commodified as a romanticized cultural object. The traditional, then, as a dialectic of constancy and fluidity of practice that has been transmitted through generations is halted and frozen in order to fulfill the state's goals of reproducing and maintaining official Balinese identity as a series of images. These pictures, which appear to move but never change, provide both a larger representation of the nation's idealized essence and a key element in the global, political economies of display and tourism.

While the violence against earlier practitioners continues, the *Jejer* and *Janger* forms have become part of Indonesia's rich and diverse folk culture, or the cultural identity of "the people." Populist dance practice, in its broadened nationalist function determined by the state, is thus granted a respected position, transformed into a supporting pillar of national integrity, one that continues to stand after the fall of the regime that erected it. During the post-Suharto *Reformasi* era, the state's claim upon these kinds of practices has in fact been further extended through the recent establishment of *Undang-Undang Intelek Properti,* as the new intellectual property laws governing the definition and performance of Indonesian traditional arts are known.

However, these laws have recently provoked criticism from certain independent Indonesian artists, as well as from major foreign institutions (such as the Ford Foundation) that have long-standing cultural projects based in the country and who, in the past, have mostly kept themselves in alignment with state policies. Of primary concern is Article 10 of *Undang-Undang 19/2002* (Government Law no. 19/2002), which declares that the Indonesian state holds copyright over the anonymous works that constitute shared or communal folk heritage. Examples of such works are stories, folk tales, legends, historical narratives, musical compositions, songs, handicrafts, choreography, dances, and calligraphy.[16]

Here, the law both protects the state's claim to certain dance practices and reinforces the state's agenda of regulation, which subsequently affects would-be dance practitioners. If a dance form itself is "protected" by law, then any effort by the original practitioners to reclaim it, requisition it, or reexamine its contextualization could face serious legal repercussions. Thus, citizens' actions and ideas regarding art forms that have been practiced within their families for generations (now including those not previously targeted by the New Order for "subversive activity") may be considered illegal by the state and classified as subversive and destructive to the nation. The concern over the effects of copyrighting traditional performances and arts has also been taken up by many scholars in the United States. Among them, the Social Science Research Council in New York has begun a collaboration with the Ford Foundation and the Law Center in Indonesia, which sent a team to investigate the state's copyrighting of traditional forms. However, as might be expected, the issue of practitioners banned, tortured, and/or vanished by state aggression was not included in the agenda for their discussion.[17]

Up to this point, my analysis of Indonesian state cultural representation has sought to establish the positioning of cultural production as a central object and mechanism of government control, resulting in a complex web of policies, rules, and standards regarding the arts. Using nationalism as a strategy, the state has legitimated its cultural reconstruction while successfully decontextualizing the practice of certain art forms, eventually reclaiming them as part of the national cultural identity. While focused on preserving cultural practice through mass reeducation, however, the cultural reconstruction process was faced with a dilemma, because many practitioners had been accused of embodying communist ideas and were therefore forbidden to practice.

Ultimately, a presentation of the cultural as emblematic of a national identity based around traditional values needed to be strategized using different regulatory mechanisms. Those dancers who were determined by the state to be free and clear of any association with the left or with those labeled *terlibat* became the new "regulatory bodies." The most highly skilled of these young, "clean" dancing bodies were selected and "institutionalized" via the lengthy national education process and then installed in state dance troupes and art institutes as guardians of the technical purity and formal decontextualization of what is now considered the state's intellectual property. In this context, they effectively function as copies of those who have gone missing, covering the gaps left by their absence as if they had never existed and therefore could not have disappeared.

Mimesis and Replica

In Indonesian dance, mimesis takes place amid the decontextualization of forms such as *Jejer* from earlier meanings and assignments of value, and from the physical locations in which they were performed and the actual bodies who performed them. For Walter Benjamin, replications of this kind functioned to strip forms and works of art of their "aura," a concept that is inextricably linked to Benjamin's understanding of authenticity: "the authenticity of a thing is the essence of all that is transmissible from its beginning, ranging from its substantive duration to its testimony to the history which it has experienced." Thus the "withering" of aura is a "process, whose significance points beyond the realm of art."[18]

For Benjamin, whose writing preceded the greatest destruction wrought by National Socialism, the mass replication of works of art gleamed with the potential liberation of the global underclasses. Yet he, too, saw in its broader effects the specter of violence and loss: "its social significance, particularly in its most positive form, is inconceivable without its destructive, cathartic aspect, that is, the liquidation of the traditional value of cultural heritage."[19] While many of Benjamin's contemporaries were likewise fascinated with the possibilities of libratory social engineering through the mass replication and distribution of revolutionary consciousness embedded in art, the years since his writing—and his tragic, early death—have unquestionably served to underscore the great potential danger in such practices. Ultimately, Benjamin was perhaps very close to the truth when he observed that "the tremendous shattering of tradition . . . is the *obverse* of the contemporary crisis and renewal of mankind" (emphasis added).[20] Reading Benjamin post–World War II (and, for me, post-1965), the essay serves to profoundly foreground the inextricable link between the potentially positive effects of the distancing or destruction of history and the manifestly tragic ones, as if they were opposing sides of the same coin.

In the context of Indonesia, the other side of the "crisis and renewal" that marked the rise of the New Order state—the mass replication and distribution of artistic practice by government forces—is a literal objectification and disembodiment of dance practices, as different bodies—specifically those not forbidden to dance, those not from certain villages, those not carrying the mark of "communism"—performed. This fundamental distinction is masked in part by the high degree of competence and artistic skill of the many new, state-deployed dancers who receive their training at the Arts Institute. The ability of these dancers to reproduce forms such as *Gandrung* and *Jejer* as simple emblems of the diversity of Indonesian performing arts is quite a feat of superior technique. The origin of *Jejer* as a traditional community practice outside of official systems of choreography or authorship functions to strengthen the state's regulation of rights to such "cultural property," preventing banned and/or marginalized practitioners from claiming any sort of specific ownership of the form. Further, the claims of state (that is, "collective," national) ownership, and the government funding that comes with such claims, are legitimized as the means necessary to save the practice from disappearing but not to save the people who performed it.

Here I base my analysis of appropriation, the dominant culture's adoption of a minority practice, on its key function within the representation of national cultural identity. As explained previously, this process of appropriation enabled cultural reconstruction through the presence and skilled performances of corporeal "replicas." Within Indonesia, the concept of traditional practice is defined in relation to state policies, which in turn are hidden or obscured behind a veil of reproduced "culture." Culture, then, as well as related concepts like tradition, can be regarded as hegemonic components of the Indonesian state ideological apparatus, which effect an "implicit displacement of the issues of class, of power, of rulers versus ruled . . . [producing] an object of ethnographic desire that no sooner discloses its contradictions—local to whom, for whom?—than it bypasses such contradictions in the name of culture."[21] This understanding of the concept of culture describes a relationship of state hegemony in which control is enacted, but is not visible as such.[22]

Seen in this context, culture is not simply an expression of local lives but an apparatus within a larger system of domination. In Indonesia, I have argued that it is Javanese court "culture" that, in its privileging by the state, holds sway over the nation's diverse groups through hegemonic over-representation. However, when cultural production occurs in a transnational context, such as the KIAS festival (*Kesenian Indonesia Amerika Serikat*—Festival of Indonesian Arts in the United States) held in Los Angeles in 1990, hegemony is renegotiated to some extent, and "culture" is transformed into a global commodity as well as a form of advertisement for itself. As displayed on the global stage, it promotes globalization through multicultural performance as well as through tourism and, therefore, engenders the commodification of traditional culture as represented by the Indonesian state. The global demand for multicultural performance, while often following from the offerings put forth by local governments, can at times, as in the case of UNESCO, also supersede these choices, creating its own trends in marketability that may inadvertently, or at times consciously, subvert the specific cultural and political machinations of nation states.

The focus on Javanese court dance as a "high," or refined, sophisticated art form and Balinese dance as mystical and religious in the service of Hindu ritual cultivates national pride in the values associated with these forms and generates propaganda disseminated abroad by the (mostly female) civil servants who perform on state cultural missions. (Other, non–state-employed female dancers living abroad must also be included, as the state claims ownership of their "national" practices and strives to regulate them.)

In Bali, many once believed that dancers serve God through their performances in the temple, which correspond with important religious events and ceremonies. After becoming internationally known through the writings and photographs of foreign artists and academic visitors to Bali during Dutch colonialism in the 1920s and '30s, this practice was gradually transformed, and special performances began to be organized for the entertainment of tourists outside of the ritually based context of the temple or village gathering.

In Java, the king was once the primary patron of dance. During colonial times, forms restricted to the context, and select audience, of the sultan's palace were also performed in honor of Dutch officials. Currently, Javanese court dance is still performed for the king, but it is also considered a lucrative attraction for both foreign and domestic tourists, one that simultaneously functions as promotion and naturalization of official Indonesian culture, much as it does on cultural missions abroad. The change in venue is directly related to the continual reconfiguration of symbol and myth within the sociopolitical context. Here, hegemony works profoundly through the enforced, unquestioning acceptance of those cultural forms designated by the state as appropriate for mass consumption in both local and global "multicultural" markets.

Within this system, the mythic power of Javanese kings, a central concept for national cultural production because of its focus on royal court dances, strongly parallels the myths surrounding Suharto's ascent to the dictatorial "throne" that he occupied throughout the reign of the New Order. Through the manipulation of popular, news, and academic media, the New Order government created a legendary hero status for the former Army general Suharto, comparable only to that once enjoyed by members of the royal families. Although several regional kings remained in place during the New Order (most prominent among them the sultan of Yogyakarta), after independence they no longer wielded real power in national political and governmental decisions, except in the realm of cultural production: the sultans of both Yogyakarta and Surakarta retained a strong say in the selection of dance forms for legitimation as part of the Javanese mystical-traditional canon. Although their absolute authority is limited to the palace context and the performances of the royal dance troupe, the kings' choices are highly influential within the state arts infrastructure. In addition, their status as symbols of Javanese-ness has long been instrumental in the state's projection of an image of a traditional yet highly sophisticated nation.

Bedhaya (the "highest" and most idealized form of court dance),[23] whose established traditional meaning is taught in elementary schools throughout Indonesia, thus becomes a means of reinforcing the common person's link to the traditional power wielded by the Javanese state. Here, the education system reinforces the mythology of the king's power as presented by the dance, and the continuing presence of the dance itself reinforces the contemporary relevance of the king's mythical stature, which is currently expressed in relation to the modern state. "Ancient" traditions are thus rendered eternal and brought under the dominion of national cultural policy discourse, serving the state both ideologically and economically. Indeed, the preservation of sacred practices and myths serves the government's hegemonic goals as the incalculable totality of local knowledge and custom is subsumed under the larger discursive category of culture.

In this context, Suharto's ceding of a certain level of power to the king in the arena of cultural production can be seen as a strategy aimed at maintaining his control over the nation-state as a whole. Through granting the king an opportunity to retain his cultural authority, especially in the compound of his own palace—a space that many Javanese still view as a locus of power—Suharto was able to strengthen his own authority. He recognized that the people's belief in, and loyalty to, the king would not disrupt his own national influence, because the king himself had previously surrendered to the idea of the Indonesian "nation," of which Suharto was the undisputed leader.[24]

In postindependence Indonesia, the royal palace was not a threat to the president because it no longer possessed any real political power; it was viewed instead as a link to the past and a symbol of Java's great cultural heritage. Cultural production within the palace had already been aligned with the nationalized court culture created by Suharto's New Order. By appearing to place a high value on Indonesian cultural heritage, the New Order was able to promote the country's identity as peaceful and "wealthy," or rich in the tradition of *adiluhung* (aristocracy). This policy also bolstered Suharto's totalizing approach to the control of Javanese society via the coexistence of the president's national government with the symbolic authority of the sultan's royal palace, especially as the king (as a citizen of Indonesia and not as the king of Java) was also a member of Suharto's own political party, *Golkar.* In this sense, Suharto was successful in establishing a broad, hegemonic political and cultural presence in Indonesia, and particularly in Java, the archipelago's long-standing center of power.

Based on this centralized, quasi-mythical conception of power, Javanese, and also Balinese, royal court culture appear quite natural in their dominant positions within Indonesian identity production, representing the historical integration of military power with a high cultural heritage and a sophisticated artistic tradition. While this gives the impression of a temporally stable and coherent country, it also gives rise to the need for limitation, both symbolic and material, of the vast cultural, artistic, and political diversity existing within the nation conceived, essentially, as a modern Javanese kingdom. To this end, the reification and regimentation of cultural practices exerted by many policies during Suharto's thirty-two years of leadership has foreclosed the struggles of many ethnically, geographically, and politically defined groups to articulate their own histories and cultural practices. In general, non–court-based, decentralized forms of cultural production and representation have been decontextualized, homogenized, and commodified before inclusion in the national cultural repertoire as export-ready state property.

As Edward Said argues,[25] representations such as these also feed the West's need for Orientalist cultural production from the Third World. However, as the Western art establishment's globalization project expands its interests to include increasing numbers of lesser-known, "endangered," and "marginal" art forms like *Jejer,* an indirect pressure has been applied to the New Order's center–periphery structure of domination, and certain dance practices once dismissed—or

Contemporary performance of *Bedhaya Babar Layar* by the Yogyakarta palace dance troupe. Photographer/copyright: Himawan.

actively suppressed—by the Indonesian state have slowly begun to re-emerge on the national cultural stage in connection with their international marketing and display by foreign organizations.

"Forbidden" dances like *Jejer,* however, in some sense merely enter a different category of target in the eyes of the state, which adapts its practice slightly in order to include, or appropriate, greater numbers of marginal groups as tokens within national culture. While this constitutes a response to forces beyond the control of the state, it is of course also a form of answer to the standardized international call for greater representative diversity under the rubric of multiculturalism. The insertion of marginal groups into Indonesian multiculturalism is no guarantee of a shift away from marginal status for artistic practitioners—in fact, it guarantees the continued marginalization of certain peoples through the process of reproduction of forms outside of the influence of those forms' historical practitioners, as illustrated by the case of *Jejer.* What is included instead—the replicated form as simulacrum—will have a similar impact and strategy in the global context, especially while the dominant form is performed by a replica body grounded in the New Order's politics of representation.

Given the ubiquitous practice of ideologically driven, aesthetic mimesis in various parts of the world, it is not surprising that many scholars have offered theorizations of mimesis and of simulacra. In this context, the French scholar Jean Baudrillard focuses on the capitalistic creation of a new "real," a "hyperreality" as opposed to a mere representation, which simulates historical reality, acting in its place and thereby obscuring the fact that history has disappeared.[26] He argues that in the realm of the arts, representation of other cultures is facilitated by the contemporary practice of industrialization of culture. Here Baudrillard views such representations (or appropriations with no connection to the "original") mainly as a result of globalization and imperialism. Yet his analysis does not critically address the concept of origin—certainly not in terms of its applicability to the traditional within colonized space—and does not explore the possibility for injustice during the process of making a "copy of a copy" or the replication of local- or state-produced replicas in the international sphere.

The case of cultural reconstruction in Indonesia, particularly since 1965, reveals violence and injustice to function not only in the naked acquisition of power, but as methods of producing certain types of simulacra in order to connect with the global sphere, which in turn helps support the presence and further production of the proffered replicas. In a broader sense, this is where the amnesia project begins for the Indonesian state, through the seductive draw of participation in the globalized world economy, promising greater access to mobility (also known as "development") at the national or governmental level. During the New Order regime, any action seen as questioning or disturbing this process was quickly thwarted, making way for the simulacra to become the dominant "new forms" that replace the previously existing ones. Yet the simulacra and the earlier forms remain politically and socially connected, with the former immersing and containing the latter in a history of erasure.

In this context, I argue the overlaid "hyperreality," despite its purported leveling and destruction of that which came before, is nonetheless inextricably tied to the historical "real," which remains embedded as collective unconscious, even as it is wiped from public discourse. Replica bodies, then, while defining the audience's perception of reality, necessarily take on uncanny resemblances to their forebears, creating flashes of vivid connection in which the unseen disappeared becomes visible, even if not always consciously readable as such. This correlation constitutes a departure from Baudrillard's mythological models, which have no connection to, or origin in, historical reality.

In Indonesia, citizens were imprisoned or killed because of their participation in cultural production. Faced with the horrible, violent reality of its own "birth" and beginnings, the Suharto regime sought to establish and continually reestablish its rule as obvious and natural, as if it had simply reclaimed an intact "nation"—along with its rich, ancient cultural traditions—after rescuing it from a long period of corruption and disturbance by outside influences (chiefly colonialism and communism). Attempting to rid Indonesia of any realities that would contest its position, the New Order's approach to both cultural and intercultural practice effectively places a gap between the understanding of local forms and communication among citizens themselves. Yet just as the so-called unruly bodies "suppressed" into the Earth have not actually disappeared, the memories of their lives and movements prior to the state's leveling of history continue to exist as displaced matter, matter that may move again in response to subtle shifts in the makeup of its surroundings, perhaps triggered by the appearance of uncannily familiar, dancing bodies.

In this context, the ideal of intercultural exchange as an altruistic "meeting in difference" is highly questionable, because it necessarily involves a further distancing: the extreme distillation of the complexities of collective experience into a tradable cultural concept. As commodity, cultural practice may appear as a tangible entity that moves quickly and globally, yet in order to do so, it often surrenders localities into "graspable" regions of geopolitical knowledge. As Rustom Bharucha suggests, the effort to achieve "a more reflective knowledge of local histories that cut[s] across the official boundaries"[27] of regions and states is necessarily highly fraught and problematic, because such a "creative unity" is always based in an existing, fundamentally unequal distribution of capital. Moreover, super-regional classifications tend to prioritize certain groups over others, lending unequal weight to those parties with more prominent social positions or who are considered more useful for projecting a particular state image.

Representing the Marginal

Returning to my analysis of the "replica" in Indonesian cultural construction post-1965, I do not, however, mean to suggest that the nation-state's "Orientalist" understandings are the only, or even the primary, influence on national or international cultural policy. Instead, I seek to demonstrate the replication of subaltern dance practice to be the result of pressures from multiple forces, each of which employs some form of violence. The replica is produced through the embodiment of practices by new bodies, simultaneously erasing the bodily presence of previous practitioners. However, the conception of an historical "original" here should not be taken to mean "untouched by foreign, Western, or dominant forms," since the representation of cultural practice always overlaps with embedded socioeconomic realities and the influence of ideology and is intimately entangled with histories of colonialism.

Considering the concept of tradition in this way, it becomes necessary to reexamine the sustainability of UNESCO's "sustainable development policies" in the arts as well as the preservation projects of other cultural institutions, such as museums, that collect and display various "world" arts and long-standing practices. As Marta Savigliano suggests, in the analysis of a cultural practice or tradition, there is no point to which one can trace the origins of an art form that has not always already been colonized.[28] Therefore, the pursuit of origin as a designated place or point in time—seeking a "pure" form with the goal of its preservation as such—is to falsify the human condition. Further, to erase, exclude, or eliminate the historical bodies who once performed certain cultural practices—rhetorically positioning them as originals to be replaced by eternalist state cultural discourse and its dancing replicas—is at the minimum a serious abuse of human rights. At worst, such actions constitute politicized mass murder, or genocide.[29]

The dance form *Jejer* does not occupy a dominant position in the nation-state's project of identity production, which, as previously stated, is allotted to Javanese court and Balinese ritual dances. However, it is included and recognized as part of Indonesia's "unity in diversity." In this context, a replicated dance form becomes a stand-in for the reality of Indonesia's rich and diverse culture, yet remains marginalized among the various models of national culture. As simulacrum, displaced and reappropriated, the form is easily detachable and thus available to be submerged within the state's larger project of marketing culture in prearranged, "unique" modular units.

In the context of globalization, *Jejer* is an exotic cultural product, an "outside world" selected for inclusion within the official register of human achievements. The promotion and framing of such forms enables Indonesia to represent itself internationally as both highly traditional and progressively egalitarian, a nonthreatening example of an assumed depth of spirit that the powerful West nostalgically desires but necessarily lacks. Thus Indonesia is internationally recognized—save for in a few, highly publicized examples such as East Timor—as giving voice to its myriad constituent groups in a fair and judicious way. In this context, the agenda of the nation-state and that of the international community are connected through the political economy of cultural practice, particularly in the realm of tourism. This is especially relevant when we consider cultural reconstruction and its emergence as a mechanism of state propaganda, exporting "nonpartisan" and "nonviolent" cultural forms, which are in fact historically entangled in colonial and political agendas.

While it is important to recognize that cultural construction has been used by the Indonesian state to dominate its citizens and access global markets—in a way clearly inspired by the strategies of colonialism—it is also possible to think of the process of cultural reinvention as potentially useful to the subaltern, who, in practicing it may, at some level, come to reject its initially alluring yet limited and proscribed "ends." Instead, she may attempt, in subtle or even not-so-subtle ways, to reappropriate it, finding and reinscribing her own history there, pulsing within the framing narratives provided by the state. Following Anna Tsing, we may take the perspective of marginalized, nondominant peoples in Indonesia and view cultural construction as a strategy to "shift, define and redefine their situations on the periphery of state power."[30] In this light, the participation of female practitioners in cultural construction may contain the potential to be reformulated as resistance, although their actions remain necessarily implicated in the system to which they set themselves in opposition.

At certain critical times, the nationalist construction of culture may also be viewed as an important task, both in terms of the process of decolonization that led to independence and the nation building of postindependence Indonesia, during which it was necessary to strengthen and unify the cultural identity of the new state. Yet under whatever conditions it occurs—in valiant struggle or repressive subjugation, perhaps also different sides of the same coin—in my analysis, "cultural construction" is a course of action with an unknown, and potentially unpredictable, outcome: its end, as we have seen, is not necessarily the precise state of affairs on which the government has staked its continued existence. The attempts of certain female practitioners to bring their voices into cultural representation can thus be seen as carrying, and having carried, not only the potential to decolonize but to disrupt the teleological, preordained goals of state and religious patriarchy. Any such disruption, however, must be understood as itself unable to carry the promise of a predictable, or even a desirable, outcome. The next chapter more closely analyzes the experience of women embedded in these systems of replication, globalization, and state identity formation, turning to questions of citizenship as a lens through which to further understand their agency—as well as its serious limitations—within these processes.

4. STAGING ALLIANCES

Cambodia as Cultural Mirror

She walks along Ton Le Sap River, her hand carrying a flower brace-
let that is often used as part of an offering in the Cambodian Buddhist
tradition. It impresses her with its taste of indigenous spirituality
mixed with nostalgia for an imagined past. Not far from the river
is the Tulsleng Museum. The building was a Vietnamese creation
during the invasion of Cambodia in the post–Pol Pot period; it is a
display of corpses, victims of genocide. Earlier, the Ton le Sap River
had offered her a different approach to political display and the horror
of the Khmer Rouge during her travel on a Japanese boat to Angkor
Wat, where the Apsara sculpture resides. Apsara, the goddess of femi-
ninity, the glamour and feminization of Cambodian state memory,
the representation of Cambodian cultural identity, the holy and the
sexualized. The memory of this sculpted form is carried in many fe-
male dancers who perform the masterpiece of Cambodian court dance
inspired by Apsara. She thinks, What a journey this is to take,
from the horror of mass murder to the elegant female body—what a
connection between the past and the new identity in which the value
of the feminine goddess is a primary resource.

In this chapter, I begin with an extended account of my own
travels to Cambodia. My research there has allowed me to form a
comparative analysis of participation in cultural production and the
relationship of aesthetic projects to the construction of nation–state

identity. The trips I have made to Cambodia, and their various contexts and purposes, have also served to broaden my personal perspective on the globalized system of diplomatic cultural exchange and border crossing. This comparison also works toward a deeper understanding of the function of replication processes in this precise historical moment, forming an important counterpoint and addendum to my argument in the previous chapter. There, my analysis suggested that active participation in performance, choreography, and the embodiment of dance technique may be the best tool available to Indonesian female dancers in negotiating the dialectic of agency and co-optation engendered by their bodily engagement with the state. I proposed that in the context of the present *Reformasi* era, the staging of traditional dances, together with the conscious addition of subtle or obvious modifications of state-defined context, appearance, or technique, can serve as a means of commenting on, criticizing, or revealing embedded layers of practices and the social situations in which they are performed. By contrast, in the present chapter my analysis of the material from Cambodia suggests that the knowing replication of "official" versions of forms and techniques, although based in a static, mythical conception of the past, may *in this case* serve to remember and to begin the process of symbolically mastering the violence of recent history. Yet such forms, and the replica bodies that practice them, remain strongly implicated in the global consumption of the exotic and the production of an illusory and violent "multicultural."

Building on this discussion, I examine the different strategies by which culture is instrumentalized and juxtaposed with concepts of national history in Indonesia and Cambodia. This mirroring of cultural location helps establish the foundation for my discussion of the citizenship of the female dancing body and its place within the nationalist and internationalist projects of both countries.

I traveled to Cambodia on a grant from the Asian Scholarship Foundation (through the Ford Foundation), planning to combine participation in the official celebration of forty years of diplomatic relations between Indonesia and Cambodia with my own research project on Cambodian Court Dance in the post–Pol Pot era. In this context, I was able to participate in an exchange program with

Cambodian dancers and choreographers, enabling me to "trade" not only dance technique but information on the role of the arts in both political and personal lives, while fulfilling my duty of representing Indonesia's national culture abroad. In addition to meeting dancers and choreographers, because of my passport and diplomatic status, I was able to gain access to the Ministry of Culture in both countries as well as to state representatives in Cambodia.

As elsewhere, in this chapter I employ my field notes and experiences from Cambodia, drawing on my memories of the past as I view them through the lens of the present, thus entering an auto-ethnographic moment through which I attempt to "see" and analyze both the performative landscape of Cambodia and the traveling, mobilized, and ever-changing replica within myself. In so doing, I aim to further reveal the multiple layers of use, mediation, and appearance of dancing bodies to reflect on my increasingly conflicting roles as a dance scholar and an Indonesian state dancer, both of which have served to motivate and facilitate the trip in different yet interconnected ways. My interpretation is forged of fragments captured at particular times and places, crystallized in the crafting of text after many months of traveling and returning home. My thoughts are framed by my efforts to find a conjunction of patterns in Cambodian and Indonesian cultural history, and are, of course, shaped by the discourses and disciplinary arguments in which I am steeped as well as my ongoing experience as a dancer and scholar. The following description was produced through my bodily somatic experience: as a body moving and dancing, traveling and writing.

The Female Body on Display

She walks along Ton Le Sap River, her hand carrying a flower brace-let that is often used as part of an offering in the Cambodian Buddhist tradition. It is the bracelet she bought on the street. The icon of the Buddha is presented everywhere along this decorated yet dirty boulevard across from the palace, distinctively marking the scenery of the Cambodian capital city. The smell of incense competes with the smell of cheap perfume from Thailand. Red Revlon lipstick, the bright colors of T-shirts saying "kitty," and the local factory product of "Famous Branch" jeans creates new ambience in the town. The white powder of Viva cosmetics covers the faces of young prostitutes, with their skinny bodies and long dark hair. They give slight smiles to the foreign men and suspicious looks to other women with Asian faces, or the tall blonde Russians—perceived as signs of threat, competition over access to these white foreigners who offer the myth of "going abroad," leaving their poor homes behind. The scene is reminiscent of certain areas of Jakarta, my own capital city, yet there, the girl rarely just wanders and looks and prefers to steer clear of such disconcerting scenes if she does. Here, while the transaction is similar, it is carried out by a slightly different cast of characters. These women face a steady stream of Land Rovers, UN crews, NGOs, Christian missionaries, and Mormons, as well as the familiar business travelers, diplomats and embassy representatives, foreign researchers, and tourists. The distinctness of these white European bodies and the significance of their presence impacts the native landscape, changes the ambience of the location on the street in Phnom Penh. Along the Ton Le Sap River, the female body is on display.

Meanwhile, tight security is arranged on every floor of the Hotel Cambodiana in Phnom Penh. It is 7:00 A.M., April 2002. The hotel guards, undercover security, and police are stationed in front of the elevator, at entrances, and in some open spaces. It is clear that an important event, such as the arrival of a guest from abroad, has been prepared. Outside the hotel on Sisowath Boulevard many young students wave flags and signs that read, "Welcome Chinese dignitaries." By the other entrance to the hotel, signs read "Long Life to the Prime Minister of India."

The visit to Cambodia by foreign leaders is tied to their nations' positions as donor countries to Cambodia since the fall of the Pol Pot regime. The arrival of Atal Bihari Vajpayee, the Indian prime minister, signals India's donation of money and rice after a flood in February 2002. In addition, Vajpayee has agreed to provide a judge for the Khmer Rouge trials in case the United Nations continues to refuse to take part in any tribunal. Moreover, agreement has been reached on the Ta Prohm temple reservation in Siem Riep, an area of Angkor Wat. The Angkor Wat complex itself has been a part of the negotiations among the Cambodian authorities, UNESCO, Japan, France, and many other donor countries interested in preservation of "traditional" space and art forms.

On this night in April 2002, Prime Minister Hun Sen will be hosting Vajpayee, while Princess Buppha Devi (the daughter of King Norodom Sihanouk, a formerly exiled member of the royal family who was voted in as constitutional monarch in 1993) will welcome the visiting Chinese dignitaries. The history of Chinese relations with the royal family in Cambodia is a long one, strengthened by the Chinese government's hosting of King Sihanouk after his exile during the war in Cambodia. In addition, Hun Sen had recently approved a Chinese government proposal regarding an electricity project (although the project is still tied up in the negotiation process in the national assembly).

On the north side of the city, next to the Funcinpec[1] political party's main office near the French Embassy, the students at the Royal University of Fine Arts (RUFA) are preparing their dance performances for the Cambodiana Hotel. The RUFA building is just across the street from the embassy and political party office headquarters, and the juxtaposition of these contending architectural symbols is striking: The French Embassy building is bright and very big, dominating the street's facades. There is a hall for meetings, dinners, and celebrations, as well as a large garden where the French ambassador's residence is located. In contrast to the structural elegance of the French Embassy, at RUFA, students struggle to clean the dirty floors. The signs of poverty and intense political turmoil, the remnants of colonialism, overshadow their arms, hands, and feet. But the vibrant dance practice manages to transform the dirty building. Some students dress up in colorful rehearsal costumes, and others start warming up by exercising their fingers, bending them back, as they've been trained, until they nearly touch their wrists. At 8:00 A.M., the teachers begin to arrive.

With just one glance from an instructor, all activity suddenly stops and the students divide into nine groups. The divisions seem to be based on age and the type of dance learned. In this school, the dancers, ranging in age from seven to twenty years old, practice together in one long dancing hall. Most of them are female, except for nine male students who are studying the monkey character, Hanuman. The monkey character, which also exists in Javanese and Balinese dance and mythology, is performed in a repertoire based on the Hindu epic *Ramayana*. However, because of the comical presentation of this figure in Cambodian variations of the story, new pieces are often created exploring the possibilities of the monkey character, whose funny, acrobatic movements are popular with local audiences, and particularly with children.

Yet the dominant presence of the female dancing body remains unchallenged, taking center stage in every performance. Even in the story of Rama and Sita, a princess and a prince, both roles are performed by female dancers. Watching the practice, I can identify all of the familiar characters in the *Ramayana:* the demon, the princess, and each of the male characters who are performed by women, with the exception of the monkey. On stage, seven male instrumentalists and three female singers play music to accompany the dancers. Off to the side of the stage, the other eight groups of students practice to a chant which resounds throughout the hall: "tak ting ting ting tak ting ting." For one hour each group rehearses earnestly, all students following the same rhythm with intense concentration.

At 9:30 A.M., Princess Bupha Devi, who is also the minister of culture, arrives accompanied by Princess Botum, who is from King Sisowath's lineage,[2] a member of the royal court who also works in the Ministry of Culture. They pull up in a Land Cruiser full of the princess's puppies. When the minister enters, all the teachers and students bow and kneel on the floor. All of their hands form the salutation sign, palms clasped in front of the chest with fingers tight together.

The gesture used for greeting an esteemed person is the same gesture used when Cambodians go to a temple to pray to the Buddha. In Cambodia, this salutation is a very common way of signaling respect for others, while, in contrast, bowing and kneeling on the floor occur only when encountering the royal family. The belief that the king is supernaturally connected to a higher power affects people's attitude toward the king and the members of the royal court. The princess, as the daughter of King Sihanouk, herself a former dancer, receives this sort of treatment not only from the faculty at RUFA but from the general public anywhere she goes in Cambodia.

With a wooden box of food, a Starbucks coffee cup from neighboring Thailand, and a cigarette in her hand, Princess Buppha Devi starts to evaluate the preparations. Her presence, together with these items, displays the evidence of a transnational commercial reality and identity. It is very unusual for a female in Cambodia to smoke in public, so the princess occasionally glances around to make sure that the official guests have not yet arrived. Starbucks coffee, which does not exist in Cambodia—the closest source is Thailand—represents the new face of the food and drink industry, which is currently tempting certain segments of this Third World country as it grows and "develops" following its long war and various internal struggles. Monivong Boulevard, at the center of Phnom Penh's industrial sector, has developed rapidly, and Western-style fast food has become commonplace. French cuisine, complete with wine and baguettes, and Thai, Indonesian, Indian, Chinese, and Vietnamese restaurants are also more abundant here than in the rest of Phnom Penh. In addition, there are Korean, Japanese, and fusion (Vietnamese-French, Thai-French, or Cambodian-French) restaurants along the Ton Le Sap River, coexisting with areas of prostitution frequented by expatriates and tourists. In Phnom Penh, the political economy of globalization is readable like a map in the city's new, hybrid commercial-public-social spaces defined by the economics of pleasure and privilege.

All the teachers are seated on the floor surrounding the princess. Some of the dancers are still in motion, while others prepare their makeup. The groups who have been dancing offstage have finished rehearsal. At the same time, a male teacher prepares a fan for the princess and six others prepare chairs and three wooden tables facing the stage, while the rest continue cleaning the hall. Two hours later, luxury cars rarely seen in Phnom Penh arrive at the university carrying the Chinese diplomat, followed closely by an open truck full of bodyguards.

Without exception, all students sit on the dirty floor, obscuring its drabness with their colorful costumes. The guests are mostly men, and the two princesses and male teachers sit in chairs. Despite my own status as an official guest, I use my relationship with the school as a visiting dance teacher to remain standing in the background, observing the scene from a slight distance. The ceremony begins with a welcoming speech by the rector of the school, Mr. Toykun, with protocol conducted in both Chinese and Khmer. Afterward, the show begins, and nine girls perform a wishing dance, flowers adorning their hands and hair, their bodies firm and childlike.

The beautiful and youthful quality of the dancers seems to transform the dirty building from a symbol of poverty, erasing the remnants of genocide and the reminders of current corruptions, replacing it with another world, one of refinement and beauty, constructed for the express purpose of welcoming the guests. During the performance, I saw what seemed to be a look of astonishment on the faces of many Chinese dignitaries.

The next day, the display is repeated, with greater pomp and circumstance, for the visit of Vajpayee, the Indian prime minister. Because of India's larger role in both Cambodian development and politics, Vajpayee would dine with Hun Sen in a far more opulent setting than the headquarters of RUFA. In early evening, Hun Sen leaves his residence on Norodhom Boulevard, where most embassies and ministry offices are located, escorted by military and police guards. He arrives a short while later at Le Royal Hotel, considered the best in Cambodia. Inside, undercover security scan the table, microphones, chairs, and walls with metal detectors again and again. The dinner seating arrangement is organized by rank over a series of round tables, except for Hun Sen and Vajpayee, whose table is long and facing the stage where the dancers from RUFA will perform. Suddenly everything becomes quiet, and the musicians and singers place themselves beside the stage. All the dancers are in a line based on the order in which they appear, while in the kitchen, an Indonesian chef from Bali, surrounded by guards, is busy coordinating the food preparations. Hun Sen enters the banquet room, abruptly preceded by the sound of Khmer traditional music. Here again, because my entrée is established through my relationship with the school of dance, I stand by the side door through which the performers will enter, observing but unseen by the other guests. For me, the scene is reminiscent of certain official events in

Indonesia when former president Suharto hosted dinners for important foreign guests.

Fifteen minutes later the prime minister of India arrives, and the entire room stands as the music plays again. Hun Sen stands and gives a welcoming speech in Cambodian. Then Vajpayee gives a speech in English, mentioning the cooperation between Cambodia and India, highlighting political and cultural connections and ongoing financial support.

The first performance begins; again a wishing dance symbolizing welcoming and offering. Again, all the dancers are female. Tonight there are eight other performances, three of them from the royal court, and five traditional forms practiced outside the court, which are labeled "folk dances."[3] The evening's centerpiece is the famed *Apsara,* the performance of which marks the official beginning of the events after all guests are seated.

The five dancers on stage are dressed in beautiful silk, with sparkling gold fabric tightly covering their upper bodies. Heavy, elaborate headdresses frame their faces and hair. The dancer in the middle moves slowly to the front, her right hand held out above the shoulder, facing the audience at an angle; the others follow. Thick gold bangles attached to dancers' legs create a particular resonance as bare feet are raised after each soundless step on the floor. Their slow, graceful march follows the rhythm of the *roneat* (a bamboo xylophone), swaying gently from side to side as dancing bodies approach the front of the stage. After the first few minutes four dancers break away and remain in the background, continuing to marching harmoniously along with the chanting of the singers. The middle dancer again takes the lead, turning with outstretched finger, as if a princess poetically commanding her servants, and the four slowly bend at the knee, coming to rest on the floor in honor of the primary dancer. Slowly each pulls a lotus flower from her belt, and standing slowly, they pose in almost deathlike stillness, their positions modeled after the goddess Apsara, whose statue most prominently adorns Angkor Wat, along with the ubiquitous reliefs of lotus flowers. Afterward, they march again in perfect synchrony for nearly fifteen minutes before leaving the stage.

When the dance is finished, the master of ceremonies suddenly stands and gives a short speech to honor the presence of Vajpayee, concluding with a reference to the possible collaboration with India on the issue of the international tribunal focused on the atrocities committed by Pol Pot and Khmer Rouge. Here, the performance of *Apsara* has been positioned to mediate a crucial moment in the functioning of the Cambodian state vis-à-vis the international community. Accordingly the emcee is careful to identify it as the most refined of court masterpieces, pointing out its connection to the famous Angkor temple, whose structure and mythical stature have also survived the ravages of ancient history and recent genocide.

As a closing to the evening's festivities, the students perform a new creation based on an Indian dance. The piece is choreographed by Ms. Somali, one of the teachers at RUFA, who learned the dance through watching a Thai TV channel that had become a popular fixture in Cambodian homes at that time. Concluding with Ms. Somali's new work, the evening was enchanting: dancing bodies, exotic cuisine representing the nations of both Hun Sen and Vajpayee, and luxurious and "ancient" costumes of gold and silk. There were no male dancers for that evening, except a short, solo performance of the monkey character. The event served its purpose and was considered a success, garnering further financial and infrastructural commitments from India, with the stated goal of helping foster peace and stability. The plan was aimed at attracting other potential investors and donor countries, putting forth a unified vision of a harmonious culture, rising anew from the ashes of destruction at the hands of communists during the Cold War.

Cultural Memory and the Female Dancing Body: Cambodia and Indonesia

In Cambodia, instead of Indonesia's official silence, I witnessed calls for "recovery" from a history of genocide—both a psychological recovery from traumatic experience and the excavation and restoration of embodied memories surviving the destruction wrought by Pol Pot. Both are sought in the beauty of Apsara, the sculpture and goddess that inspired the court dance of Cambodia. In this context, Apsara was both a reconstructed myth and identity and a symbol of survival for many. This is the path that I trace, where the resources of state development projects are intimately connected to the female dancing body, and where the display of this body—next to evidence of the human capacity for self-destruction that calls to be (re)developed—remystifies it, offering an enduring, exalted, and resistant identity.

As the victim of a more recent, internationally recognized genocide at the hands of a movement that identified itself as communist, Cambodia possesses a direct, unassailable connection to the interests of much of the post–Cold War international aid community. Its display of dancing bodies also seems to dovetail rather perfectly with this interest, as it represents a central, royal and traditional practice that was a documented target of the Khmer Rouge and thus constitutes a clear resistance to its influence, which at this point takes the form of a recovery from the damage done. The binary sense of good and evil, and of the absolute "good" of economic and infrastructural aid and investment is established by the fact of a known "evil" that has for the most part been eradicated. Even currently communist nations such as China can help out without any seeming contradiction; the Khmer Rouge are well-enough established as cold-blooded killers, and combating the lingering effects of their rule in Cambodia may help to polish China's own image internationally.

Thus, while the female dancing body is a symbol and vehicle of ongoing national recovery projects in both Cambodia and Indonesia, it must necessarily function differently within each context; Cambodia's method of display, showcasing the horrors of recent history alongside the beauty of a semi-mythical past, is in some ways antithetical to the Indonesian state's approach. There, in addition to official cultural events, we find a series of sites not unlike theme parks, displaying an idealized version of history and national harmony: Taman Mini in Jakarta (an actual theme park consisting of a miniaturized version of the archipelago, showcasing the dance and traditional architecture of many Indonesian ethnic groups alongside monorails and costumed employees bearing suspicious resemblance to Disney characters), the "preserved" Balinese villages in Tenganan, the contemporary museum of Balinese fantasy Garuda Wisnu Kencana, or the exhibits of "ancient" art in private galleries, former palaces, and any number of resorts and tourist hotels. Taken together, these sites collaborate with dancing bodies to distort and hide the violence of the past, offering up pure, glorified aestheticism for the public's consumption and delight.

In contrast, yet similarly related to agendas of the Western-led international community, Cambodia displays its background of horror, poverty, and genocide in clear view. While victims may find such memories extremely disturbing, particularly in the context of the economic struggles of the present, the state policy of openness regarding past violence and victimhood has attracted significant attention to the need for economic development and rebuilding. The support Cambodia has received since Hun Sen H. E. Samdech's rise to power has been made possible in part by the effectiveness of the state's policy of distancing itself from the Pol Pot regime. Despite a significant amount of continuity between the former Khmer Rouge leadership and the current government, it has successfully positioned itself in opposition to the horrors of the past, disclaiming any responsibility. Along with many other Western powers, the U.S. government has helped legitimize this distinction through various means. For example, in December 1996, Hun Sen, second prime minister of the Royal Government of Cambodia, was given the World Peace Prize by its California-based award council for his great and active contribution to the peace process and the recovery of his people and to national reconciliation and development in Cambodia.

Indonesia: Mimicry of the "Enemy"

In Indonesia, however, what is purportedly being recovered from is far murkier, because the PKI, unlike the Khmer Rouge, was eliminated more than forty years ago and there have been no recorded attempts to revive it. Further, Indonesia's "aid" comes largely in the form of foreign investment and manufacturing, which has been flowing in from the West and elsewhere since the time of the killings. Yet from its inception, the New Order's survival at home—and its position among the international community, where its success as a recipient of investment and foreign aid heavily depends on its historical self-representation and its Cold War–based political alignment—

has relied on allusions to the presence of an immanent, evil enemy: an insidious, murderous communist force—not unlike the Khmer Rouge—latently hiding within its own citizenry, ready to strike at any time if not suppressed through continual vigilance on the part of the state.

In 1965, Suharto and the military made a show of eradicating this illusive "subversive" force by killing millions of citizens whom they claimed were the embodiment of its massive, and as of yet unrealized, potential to wreak havoc on the nation. Yet because this "evil" was never really visible in the first place—the PKI never engaged in mass killing or provided evidence of planning to do so—a "clean kill," as in the defeat of the Khmer Rouge, where bodies, museums, and trials came to symbolize a complete break with a historical "bad guy," was neither empirically possible nor ideologically desirable for the New Order. (They did, however, create a monument and museum depicting the killing of the seven officers on September 30, 1965, attempting to establish a link between this event and the "potential" for mass killings by the PKI.)

For thirty years, then, the legitimacy of the Indonesian state was dependent on a paradox: the conception of Indonesia as a nation that was in many ways completely under government control and yet was simultaneously in a constant state of alert against the reemergence of a fabled, subversive force; a force that, like the Khmer Rouge, fit the relevant international community's definition of "evil." This position, while ideologically effective, is of course also fragile and risky, as it is belied by the fact that, given even a cursory examination of the events of recent history, the only empirical evidence of evildoing or murderous acts would point directly to the deeds of the New Order itself. Yet despite a few important calls for a more critical reaction, the Western-led international community was largely unified in its decision to support and play along with Suharto's charade. From its inception, after all, the New Order was able to provide a pleasurable, "exotic," and profitable place for international powers to engage in the business of investment, development, and "recovery."

In this context, the replica female dancing body plays its most important role, as an ever-present symbol of the "pure" essence of the nation, and of the innocence and productivity of tradition, signaling the urgent need for its preservation. In this sense, both the Indonesian and Cambodian dancing bodies perform a similar dualistic function: ensuring that national culture—as heritage—appears potent and resistant, having emerged unscathed from an endless array of battles, historical change, and potential tainting by outside influences since time immemorial. Yet, like its visually delicate, "pure" practitioners, culture must simultaneously give the impression of weakness and vulnerability, of needing to be saved from corruption at the hands of the evil, murderous, communist outsider within. This similarity of conceived function continually impressed itself into the memories I carried home from my travels to Cambodia.

From Monopedal Aesthetics to *Wajib Lapor:* The Particularities of Indonesian Strategies for "Recovery"

She feels someone push her from behind and turns around. A man, seated on the ground, raises his right hand up and asks her for money, a common scene in the city of Phnom Penh. The position of his body reminds her of a section in the Cambodian court dance when a prince demands special attention from a princess. Both bodies then lie down on a piece of wood, seemingly comfortable with each other, using a highly refined pose to describe desire. The push and stylized posture shape the female in a particular position and location on stage that does not read as violence to the body because of the aestheticization of the experience; rather, it lends an artistic value that carries the action through. We forget the body's horrifying history in that moment because of the sublimation and glamorization of its presence. In contrast, the man seated on the ground outside the palace has only one leg. His body is straight, and he insists on getting her attention, while on stage "the prince" insists upon "the princess." Unlike the court dancers, the man's lack of glamour or costume, the absence of stylization to his body, perhaps fails to elicit an effort to understand, and therefore risks being ignored, lost in the surroundings. Yet ironically, the display of this man's single, visible leg, marked with gunshot holes, pulls me back further to the words of Amitav Ghosh and a scene he describes aboard the Amiral-Kersaint *during an early French encounter with*

the presentation of Cambodian dancing bodies at the 1906 Exposi-
tion Coloniale in Marseille. Here as well, certain abstracted body
parts became a major focus of public attention: "The whole deck was
a blur of legs, girls' legs, women's legs, 'fine, elegant legs,' for all the
dancers were dressed in colorful sampots which ended shortly below
the knee."[4]

Like their contemporary counterparts in post–Pol Pot Cambodia, the exposed legs of these elegant dancers reveal a fetishistic projection of the female body, broken down into symbolic elements that perhaps confirm the expectations of viewers, as primed by the lucrative market in paintings, photographs, and films featuring the (more often than not female) colonial Other and distributed throughout Western Europe and the United States. In the Javanese court, the main source for the official display of the female dancing body in Indonesia, a similar yet modified approach is employed. Here, the woman is wrapped with a special cloth, shaping the body while covering it from ankle to chest.

In some cases the Javanese dance symbolizes the king's sexual relations with the mythical figure known as the queen of the South; the swathed dancers provide a ritual connection, acquiring a mystical sexual meaning. A batik cloth called *kemben* is often used for the upper part of the costume to further define the abstracted female body represented by the dancers. The *kemben* seems to change the dancers' bodies, accentuating the breasts, chest, and buttocks, making them appear larger. The costumes for women in Javanese court dance also include a skirt, or sarong, which, like the *kemben*, is made of hand-painted batik. During the Dutch occupation there were many changes to the costumes, such as the added use of velvet to cover the upper body. However, certain basic techniques and rules of Javanese court dance, such as using only one leg to hold the weight of the body, have, since before the time of the Dutch, served the aesthetic, symbolic needs of those in power and thus remained largely unmodified. The condition of this particular leg, which silently bears the weight, and the ensuing effect on the female body—an important stylistic idiom of Javanese court dance—is taught, transmitted from one generation to the next, and therefore considered "traditional."

A performance of *Srimpi Gambir Sawit* at Pakualaman Palace, Yogyakarta.
Photographer/copyright: Himawan.

In the context of performing abroad, the monopedal female
dancing body becomes a common signifier of cultural difference,
since Javanese court dance dominates presentations for Indonesian
state cultural missions. Poised, and balanced on one leg, the Javanese dancing body plays her contemporary role in the display of
Otherness: a show enabling the establishment of global alliances
that proffer a more spiritual, essential, or "human" engagement and
knowing, hiding the underlying governmental transactions. The
replica dances a cultural form categorized as "Third World." Her
particular world, however, includes refined, courtly arts that suggest
its sacred, ancient origins, the position and value of which are assumed to have remained constant since a time before memory. The
same can be said of Cambodian court dance; both courts, which are
often meant to allegorize their nations as a whole, mediate history
and identity through the body, and the body through the ritualiza-
tion of presentation.

Wajib Lapor: "Treatment" and Global Concern

The experiences of dancing and of seeing the wounded body of the beggar are for her connected in a linear way by the memory of violence. The vanished coexist in the surviving bodies of the wounded and then slowly disappear into the depths of memory as the trained and uniformed citizens—the military officer, civil servant, or state dancer—come to dominate daily life. She thinks of her adoptive father, to whom she owed so much for sending her to school, who fought in the independence movement and the "communist clash" in Madiun.[5] *Her aunt, who claimed to be her mother and was the unofficial wife of her adoptive father, had lost many members of her own extended family through such "disappearances." Along with those missing, the government had accused her aunt-mother of being a communist because she performed for Gerwani. Now, along with several other "unclean" relatives, her aunt made a weekly trip to the local military office, where she was required to be "checked up on." This obligatory demonstration of submission to the local authorities, and, by proxy, the state, was known as* wajib lapor.

During such periodic absences of adult women at home, she often heard gamelan *(a type of metallophone-based Javanese music) coming from the house of a former Nationalist Party leader who became the headmaster of her school. Many children from the village, she among them, paid daily visits to his house, which was big enough to study and practice the court dance* Bambangan Cakil *(an excerpt from the* Mahabharata*). She learned to use the* keris *(dagger), staging fierce yet elegant duels as her movements were said to be guided by the ancient Hindu epic. The dance taught at the headmaster's home describes the story of the prince of Janaka and his battle with a demon creature called Cakil. Janaka is famous as a hero, and whoever performs this dance must be aware of the appropriate posture and facial emotion in order to respect his character. Although she loved this dance, and it was exciting to learn how to fight and resist an attack, she was always scared if she did not remember the sequence correctly; the teacher would beat with a stick those who did not remember.*

And often, in the middle of a dance rehearsal she had to stop, frozen by the sound of a young man's repeated screams: "Don't kill, don't fight, there's blood everywhere and too much dancing!" Most students were afraid of that young man, including her. She would run and not come back until the teacher came looking for us. The young man who was the source of our fear, one of the headmaster's sons, was said to have gone mad, a categorization that these days might land him in a local treatment or recovery program for PTSD (posttraumatic stress disorder). Yet for this boy, there was no doctor or healing project available, because his condition was outside the purview of national or global concerns over health. His sickness was a type of corporeal memory, the embodiment of events to which he had been a witness. Perhaps our dance reminded him of a time in that village when many dancers were killed, or maybe the use of daggers in our performance called forth memories of some other violent scene he had happened upon. Whatever the source of his outcries, they resulted in his body being forcibly secluded from public spaces, lest his memory pull others back with him into the stained fabric of recent history. Reflecting on the young man later in life, she suspected the corporeal traces of what he'd witnessed were hidden for political reasons, his categorization as a "crazy," unreliable, or sick person negating the possibility that he might someday testify or give evidence of what he had seen in a legal context. Here she learned to recognize the sickly smell of betrayal.

After 1965, the New Order government's national development project focused on a broad, grassroots approach to democracy, building cottage industries in domestic space, improving gross national product, and moving "forward," while clearly attempting to leave certain things behind, such as the young man who had gone "mad," my aunt and other relatives, those who were required to report to local military offices, those overlooked by nongovernmental organization (NGO) testimony and healing projects that focus on natural disasters and terrorism and others who experience continued violence to their bodies; all of these people constitute the undesirable past.[6] If they were to be included in the process of development, it would most likely be the result of projects whose nets were cast widely enough to reach them inadvertently. Primarily concerned with the immediate fallout from bombings, earthquakes, and tsunamis, the political landscape underlying and predating such events, shot through with vague, shadowy, yet powerful concepts like *wajib lapor,* is largely invisible to the international community and its interests in the Third World.

For the New Order, *wajib lapor,* which translates rather innocuously as "duty to report," functioned as a conveniently unfathomable mechanism for the control and political "rehabilitation" of civilians. As such, it could be viewed as the state's version of an NGO treatment and recovery program, whose direct concern was to manage and suppress the visibility of such underlying landscapes. Those visiting the Army office were required to listen to a speech from the officers about moral values based on the state ideology, *Pancasila,* and then repeat their promise to be faithful to these nationalist ideals. Many were forbidden to dance, sing, or carry out other artistic practices, because the state deemed certain forms of expression to be threatening to national unity. However, the weekly encounters with the Army officers often had far harsher consequences for females, many of whom were repeatedly raped and abused without the possibility of legal or other recourse. This happened most frequently in cases in which a husband had vanished, and the wife was thus forced to report to the officers alone.[7]

In Bali, the experience of *wajib lapor,* reporting to the *kelian* (head of village) or village *adat* (customary law) officers, while officially concerned with the reindoctrination of "subversives," was in fact laying bare the inner workings of the Hindu-based power structure, thus further demystifying the status of state and local authority for those who were targeted and called in for ideological treatment. As local representatives of power, many heads of Balinese villages also presided over ritual offerings and purifications embedded in official political functions. The offerings used in such rituals, which vary from small baskets of flowers to towering, intricately arranged collections of food and decorative objects borne on the head, had always been constructed with great skill by the hands of local women. In Bali, the massacres of 1965–66 were often carried out by local militias organized by village officials under the indirect command of the military. Thus, Balinese women who fell victim to rape and murder during this time were often singled out or targeted on the orders of the same local officials who ritually processed the women's offerings.[8]

After the mass killings stopped, the performance of artistry by women in the construction of offerings for official events (as well as for frequent, "strictly religious" occasions) continued to occur, producing exact replications of the forms as defined by customary law. But this work was now carried out by the hands of different women, those who had escaped murder or suspicion of connections to the left, those who were not required to perform the new ritual called *wajib lapor.*[9] Here, the beauty of the offerings, and the ancient Hindu rituals' official function of blessing and cleansing village events, promoting peace and harmonious existence, serve to obscure or cast doubt on the likelihood of the stories of some of its practitioners' suffering.

Like the female dancers in my own childhood village who were "lucky" enough to have survived the killings, many of the women I met in Bali told me they frequently experienced rape and sexual abuse during 1965 and the years that followed, after they or their husbands were accused of connection to the Communist Party (PKI) or left-leaning organizations such as Gerwani. As with the case of dancers and artists, the women's crafting of offerings and performance of bearing them to public ceremonies while dressed in traditional costume was banned and performed by other bodies. The bodies of the accused women, considered a threat to the purity of the rituals, were instead sent as "offerings" to the local authorities, so that they might be "cleansed" within the walls of the regional military or village headman's office. Thus the female body performs the continuous function of mediating the transition from violence and chaos to state reidentification; whether as sublimated dancer, as a means of sexual placation, or as aesthetic adornment, the moving, performing female body represents the promise of recovery for a nation-state that is nonetheless always necessarily in the *process* of cultural and political reinvention. Her presence inscribes a space in which national struggle is aestheticized and then crystallized within broader understandings of tradition while being consumed by citizens and visitors from far-flung provinces and states. Yet as in Cambodia, the space of the female dancer in Indonesia is unable to escape from the violence that shapes it and fills it with memory and movement.

Balinese Barong Dance: Ideology, Tourism, and the "Enemy Within"

Every morning in Bali a crowd of mostly foreigners gathers outside an open stage, located within the complex of a fairly large temple. The temple itself is exclusively used for local religious practice (although tourists, as in most other places in Bali, are welcomed to walk in and out of ceremonies, provided they wear some minimal ritual attire such as a belt or sarong over their regular clothes). The stage, however, covered with paintings of Balinese religious imagery, is filled twice a day, 365 days a year with tourists (no sarong required), who pay to watch an excessively violent version of a ritual performance known as the *Barong* dance. Although there are many venues in Bali for *Barong,* this particular show prides itself on an "authentic replication" of the ritual of suffering performed in temples, during which dancers become possessed, impressing razor-sharp *keris* (ceremonial daggers) into their chests, which somehow never break the skin or draw blood. The scene is performed immediately after the "actual" (within the context of the show's narrative) killing of Rangda, the witch and ultimate symbol of evil, whose existence is conceived as the dark side of the dualistic Balinese Hindu philosophy, the *Rwa Bhineda.*

According to the local villagers, many former "perpetrators"— those assisting the military and local authorities in their combined effort to identify and eliminate suspected communists during the mass murders of 1965–66—have become members of various *Barong* troupes and that they can be identified by their especially gruesome renditions of the show. (I have no direct evidence, however, that members of the troupe I am describing are former killers; in any case, a good portion of them are too young to have participated in the violence during Suharto's rise.) Interesting, however, despite its basis in capitalist practice and disconnection from the sacred space of the temple, I am also told by the director[10] that this particular *Barong* performance is always "real." This assertion is based on the dancers' claims of *actually* becoming possessed (and actually trying—applying real pressure—to force the *keris* into their own chests), as opposed to simply pretending for the sake of the tourists and the ticket sales they represent. In addition to the *keris* section, the show graphically depicts the murder of the witchlike Rangda, along with the torture and mutilation of her followers, in ways eerily similar to both falsified state reports of leftist violence *and* testimony regarding the fate of local victims of state-aligned militias during the mass killings in 1965–66.[11]

This *Barong* performance, then, presents an "authentic" imitation of temple-based ritual stabbing, while simultaneously framing and interpreting the type of violence that took place outside of temples in 1965 in terms of an absolute binary of good and evil. The relevance of such a binary, bolstered by the embeddedness of local Hindu practice in daily and political life, is perhaps its mimetic positing of historical violence as a reaction to the presence of an absolute evil, a force that must be eradicated through heroic sacrifice in order for life, and nation, to continue. Like Javanese court dance elsewhere, in the context of Bali the *Barong* dance aligns traditional practice with the state's self-serving vision of history as an endless binary struggle. The participants, then, as they are figured by local sources, act as both symbolic *and* empirical and historical "erasers," having ended the lives of citizens in 1965 and subsequently submerged the specific, embodied experience of murder within the naturalized practice of traditional culture, simultaneously obscuring it and lending it the mythic status of a universal struggle between dark and light. Performed for tourists, their dance is meant to take on the aura of an unbroken continuum of spiritual practice, which the purchase of a ticket will help to preserve. Yet in the context of the Balinese village where it is performed, it serves as a coded reminder of the violence that took place and that threatens to return if anyone deigns to disturb the ruling order.

In Bali, the ubiquitous image of Rangda, a vicious witch with a wild shock of unruly white hair, huge fangs, and pendulous breasts was also frequently used after 1965 as a representation of members of Gerwani, the left-leaning, protofeminist women's group that was one of the most "high-value" targets during Suharto's campaign of terror. As discussed in earlier chapters, in the media, Gerwani members were alleged to have participated in the killing of seven high-ranking military officers on September 30, 1965 (the September 30th Movement, claimed by Suharto and the military to be an attempted coup d'état, which became known as "G30S-PKI"), enacting a bloody, ritualistic dance in which they amputated the officers' genitals. Within the *Barong* dance, the murder of Rangda enacts the symbolic rescue, or perhaps "rehabilitation," of female characters that she has possessed, purportedly allowing them—as *wajib lapor* is claimed to do for former members of Gerwani—to return to their culturally normative functions within the patriarchal Hindu hierarchy portrayed in the story. When the violence has run its course and the dance is nearly finished, the exorcism of the "evil," subversive spirit of Randga from the female characters is signified by the re-entrance of the glamorized, "pure" female dancing body to the stage.

In the context of this particular *Barong* performance, as replicated daily outside of the temple, the flashy, action-filled "stabbing" dance—already engaging state discourse on multiple levels locally—fluidly enters the global market through tourism. Here, the female dancing body, as both tourist attraction and signifier of order, becomes the symbolic glue holding together the fractured, fragmented historical reality of Bali, shaping it into a presentable whole. In so doing, she enacts another kind of recovery, drawing international recognition and investment in cultural engagement and preservation, which flows to both performers and historical victims: the villagers on whose land the show is held. Thus, the woman I spoke with who was repeatedly raped during her state-ordered *wajib lapor* visits after 1965, and who owns a small *warung* behind the performance space, now receives regular business because of the *Barong*.[12] Yet the "ordered" reality presided over by the female dancing body remains tenuous, fragile, and threatened by embodied memory, waiting for the chance to show itself, to respond to the violent scene replayed daily in the backyard of its victims and their children.

In contexts such as this, whether deployed by the governments of Cambodia, Indonesia, or certain other nations in the region, the female dancing body becomes an icon, a commodity and a celebration, a tool in political bargaining and diplomacy. On tour, or displayed for visiting dignitaries, the specificity of each body is easily shed, becoming interchangeable to suit the purposes of globalization and marking nationalized culture. The body as stand-in, or fluidly translatable replica, is both detachable and reattachable to ongoing struggles or previous violence and the political contexts that drive them. Its economic role may not be as clearly readable as those bodies along the streets of Jakarta or the banks of the Ton Le Sap River, yet its potential power and mobility are greater, precisely because of its embeddedness in the nation-state's emergent political and economic identity.

As I argue in the next chapter, the *value* placed on the female dancing body—the nation-state's great, perceived *need* for its presence and cooperation—is precisely what enables the citizenship of the female dancer or choreographer to become "flexible." However, the potential to utilize such flexibility for resistance becomes a delicate balancing act that continually risks undermining its own mobility, safety, and viability in both the national context and on the global stage.

5. VIOLENCE
AND MOBILITY

Autoethnography of Coming and Going

She arrives alone in Cambodia from the United States with her luggage full of Indonesian dance costumes, fully funded and with a guided travel route; the grant distributor, entitled "Asianizing Asia," publicized the travel project online. Her journey is not contained within the global South, like her citizenship, but moves from West to East, as did the colonial travel of the old days. Yet her journey now has pre-acknowledgment; it is expected, as an introduction to the politics of neighborhood and regionality within the international mechanism of states' good governance in postcolonies.[1] The Cambodia in which she arrives has become an internationalized zone within UNTAC[2] and is in the process of becoming a part of the Association of Southeast Asian Nations (ASEAN). Using a special port of entrance in connection with diplomatic relations in Southeast Asia, she is greeted with an official welcome by the Dharma Wanita *representatives from the Indonesian embassy in Cambodia.[3]*

The representative, also an Indonesian woman, greets her with a smile and whispers, "Not so different from home." (The voice reminds her of a CNN advertisement on Asian tourism in which the actress Michelle Yeoh promotes Malaysia as "just another Asia," offering the tourist destination as "a home.") Accordingly, she need not stand in line at the immigration office in Phnom Penh, because the blue passport issued her gives her official status.[4]

Most female dancers who are civil servants rarely travel alone; rather, they are usually sent in large groups due to the number of performers needed for each cultural mission. The Asian female artist's dancing body is her tool on these trips and the key to her "feminized mobility," without which the coveted status of dancer and female civil servant would be lost. Her alliance with the Indonesian state confers the privilege to defy the authority of Asian borders. She brings layers of gender and class-based arrogance, leaves behind all the male officers, and raises the feminist flag. She travels alone, and in doing so she confronts patriarchy at home. Her presence is part of an evening of cultural presentation designed to commemorate the diplomatic relationship between Cambodia and Indonesia. She will be dancing, expected to represent the richness, unity, and diversity of Indonesian culture among the "neighborhood" of ASEAN nations.

The Politics of (Dis)Entanglement: A Rock and a Hard Place

In this chapter, I reflect on the fraught, liminal nature of trying to follow an increasingly critical, politicized line of discourse and thought while continuing to reap the benefits of civil service to an authoritarian state (and those of scholarship and performance within the often-rigid Western academic and arts establishments). I begin by analyzing the conditions under which Indonesian nationalized bodies are able to travel and communicate with global arts alliances. I examine the complexities of participation in the sphere of "world cultural awareness" and how to dance within a performed nation-state cultural identity that functions to mediate the state's agenda in the international sphere. Here I follow Marta Savigliano and Achille Mbembe in their discussion of the specifics of the "postcolony," in which tradition and cultural representation figure heavily in the interdependent relations between current, imperial powers and relatively new, decolonized states.[5] Although contemporary performance on the global stage seems to suggest the incorporation—or perhaps even the surrender—of traditional art forms into modern and postmodern genres (by not naming the historical specificity in order to be accepted as universal), still the Otherness, the postcolonial tradition of Indonesian performing arts, remains valuable as a source of aesthetic difference (although it is not necessarily acknowledged as such) in this category of "new arts."

The implementation of court practice as emblematic of national culture encourages the forgetting of pain through providing class-based privilege to its practitioners while vanishing the possibility of justice for historical violence and claiming millions of lives as a fair price for the (re)founding of an ancient "nation" within the "new" *world* order of neocolonialist imperialism. The basic premise of my examination in this book is that the Indonesian nation-state has a specific agenda of cultural construction, which certain female practitioners attempt to mediate in complex ways stemming from the entanglements of local position and mobility: they begin by negotiating their roles at home, struggling with the patriarchal structures of power that both constrain their lives and practice and enable them to move. Yet when they reach the apparent freedom and glamour of the global stage, they are frequently pushed back toward the generalized position of national cultural representative by the expectations of the Western-dominated sphere of world dance and its need for easily assimilable—and sellable—difference. Thus, female performers with access to mobility must mediate the expansion of state power through their own co-optation, as dancing bodies, within the capitalist context of the global stage. While these performers obtain a certain agency from their central location within multiple spheres of control, their situation, of course, is not ideal. In reality, many of them continue to live lives of daily struggle, despite their hard-won positions challenging the absolute dominance of men at the top of the national education and performing arts hierarchy.

In the current, post-Suharto era of *Reformasi,* most female performers in Indonesia remain outside the national educational system; if they do not have income from another form of employment such as factory work, housework, or selling goods in traditional markets, they face harsh social prejudice. Also, artists not affiliated with the system—those who are not the state troupe members or civil servants—who try to perform and tour independently within the local context are sometimes considered "low class" and categorized as *Ronggeng* or *Tandak* (types of street dances), labels frequently associated with the practice of prostitution. Others, especially those participating in theater performances in the capital city, Jakarta, may attempt to subvert the dominance of the national system of performing arts by visibly aligning themselves with global development agencies critical of government policy (for example, choreography that exposes domestic issues of AIDS/HIV or environmental problems to local audiences); these artists may be considered "left-wing" or politically subversive and possibly targeted by state censors or conservative or fundamentalist religious groups alike. Alternately, there are artists who travel from village to village who are associated with neither state nor cosmopolitan theater space, and are not influenced by the language of international concerns. (An interesting example of this nonaligned type could be a rural troupe that chants the story of a local goddess, providing a text of gender resistance, yet remaining anonymous and unknown within the academic world—local or global—of feminist praxis.)

Such artists can be seen as "subaltern," as they are excluded from Indonesia's official nation-state identity and from any national narratives regarding progressive female concerns. Yet it is important to view the subaltern as a complex, historical being, rather than simply a theorized shadow: Gayatri Spivak, in "Inscription: Of Truth to Size," suggests that the space of the subaltern is not "uncontaminated by the West"—even "unofficial" dancers are affected by the global system and its presence within the local.[6] In this context, the village dancers must also mediate their "speaking" in comparison to a complex set of alliances and international concerns, not only ideologically, but also in terms of survival through labor: their singing and dancing must compete with the ubiquitous presence of radio, television, Internet, and other broadcast media.

In the context of the state arts infrastructure, such subaltern artists are viewed as practicing forms that are low class or even unrecognized. However, I argue that this improvisatory space may provide a critical space for local expression concerning gender politics, discourses that are often received as humorous and unthreatening to the status quo. Yet such improvised spaces and rural mobility are not always received with warm support by the community: in certain cases the appropriateness of public gender discourse is subject to more stringent controls through both tacit and explicit collaborations of religious and state control. Further, if such forms were to gain broader recognition or be performed by intellectual groups outside of the state's network of alliances, they would likely be considered politically subversive. The existence of such women and their artistic or cultural practices are not valued within the political economy of replicas and amnesiacs that informs the construction of national culture. They must compete with other forms in order to exist, yet remain largely "under the radar," functioning without the support of cultural institutions. Here, a particular category of "speech" emerges out of a class structure that defines practitioners through capitalism yet offers limited access to negotiate its terms. In contrast, women in alliance with the state are more likely to be granted access to negotiate their mobility, in some sense because of their "usefulness" within the system that co-opts them. The greatest hope, then, lies in the potential creation of a third body, the postnationalist dancing body, which may embrace the global stage while retaining a greater level of autonomy—eventually reducing her dependence on alliance with the state—and thus a certain potential to resist co-optation. This theme, the ideal of the third body, could perhaps be said to constitute the central, structuring paradox of my book and of significant portions of my career.

Mobility and Cultural Resistance

Focusing on female dancers employed by the state, I explore the ways in which the agency of the female dancing body is created and made possible through participation in dancing as an act of speaking, not only in terms of access to spaces for performance and expression but also to different styles of dance and the possibilities they may open for the creation of alternate content. Yet I argue that women who become representatives of state cultural discourse are also subjected to the gaze of exoticism, which is operant (ubiquitously) within the global economy. Participation in international trade (often within the category of "development") is also part of the agenda of the nation-state, and women and their cultural practices are co-opted to serve this global capitalist goal; whatever mobility is gained through participation in national cultural construction opens alliances with the global economy. This relationship connects local and global forces in the formation of hegemonic identity and in the valuation and categorization of women's citizenship.

"Cultural (re)construction" was developed with the support of civilians in Indonesia, civilians who still possessed the memory of resistance to colonial rule through establishing, performing, and protecting cultural difference. In establishing Indonesia as a single nation, these same sentiments were harnessed and used to demand the loyalty of citizens. The construction of culture, when embodied by dancers, then, supports the project of nationalizing, but it also by design offers dancers access to mobility within the state structure, enabling them to mediate the state's self-representation and, to some extent, the absolute dominance of patriarchy at home. Within the context of a cultural mission abroad, the reproduction of these dynamics informs the complex and contradictory nature of the offering up of culture for export. Similar accounts have been discussed by Marta Savigliano in the context of Tango (in Japan and the West) and Naima Prevots, who documents the role of the U.S. State Department in promoting American artists within a particular history of Cold War intercultural relations.[7]

As was the case for my fieldwork in Cambodia (detailed in the previous chapter), this cultural export is frequently performed in order to establish a new diplomatic relationship or expand an existing one, which then translates into economic cooperation between a sending and a host country. The idea is that by promoting culture in a way that is focused on beauty in connection with a sense of peaceful harmony, investors or major donor countries will feel safer in pursuing stronger economic ties. (Performance of traditional arts also functions as a particular political, economic tool: dances appear to reveal the "human side" of state representatives and their national traditions, playing on the desires of donor nations to know their Others and possibly fostering a sense of emotional attachment that may extend and strengthen future relations.)

For the mostly female practitioners involved, cultural missions (or self-exportation) offer a chance for mobility through financial earnings; generally the compensation for dancers traveling abroad is based on the host country wage standards. If the mission is sponsored by the Indonesian consulate or other official channels, the salary, though paid in Rupiah, will still be higher than that of performers within the country. Moreover, the artist-resident abroad also gains a channel through which to build and exercise mobility. Southeast Asia is one of the regions officially considered to be a destination for promoting American culture and foreign policy in the post–Cold War period. This has put in motion several processes that enabled the performances and cultural practices of Indonesia to cross borders and be exported to the United States.

There are also cases in which neighboring countries, such as Singapore, India, Korea, Cambodia, or Thailand, have become the destination of Indonesia's export culture (tourism) and cultural exchange programs, creating interlocal alliances and artistic "politics of neighborhood" within the nondominant spaces of Asia, and particularly Southeast Asia. (Usually such alliances take the form of workshops, collaborative performance, or conferences.) Yet even culture-for-exchange projects within Asia still rely on wider, global spheres of cultural trade, because the entire phenomenon is largely predicated on the availability of funding and networking mediated by the most prominent arts foundations, nearly all of which are based in the United States and Europe. As a lower priority for most state cultural agendas, such projects provide fewer opportunities for female artists to participate, yet the theoretical (and occasionally actual) existence of these more "interlocal" spaces nonetheless serves as a goal on which the sights of many practitioners are set. Thus, the politics of representation are established across a complex web of connections, some of which serve to obscure the powerful hand of the nation-state and the constant pull of global capital on all involved.

In the era of globalization, the rise of conservative traditionalist or fundamentalist Islamic movements within the local context can be correlated in certain, important ways to the strategic need for new, modern nation-states to export culture, which requires the participation of citizens, particularly females, on behalf of the state. This cultural exportation mediates and expands the role of women, although it does so in a way that is limited by the parameters of the economics

of cultural labor. In the case of Indonesia, the pressure of global economic competition and imperialist modes provides both cultural and
domestic or "guest-worker" labor for large numbers of women, thus
raising a number of potential issues for conservative Islam. In the
case of nonperformers, the distribution of labor through women's
guest-worker programs (and also prostitution) is connected to this
space of participation, where women's bodies become commodified
and are often viewed as a *kodrat*, or "fallen." Various Islamic groups
have also frequently expressed disdain for women's cultural work as
dancers—whatever the level, rural or state representative—as well
as for a number of traditional cultural practices in general. While
the stated goal of such positions is to help women who indeed often
find themselves in difficult or compromised circumstances, as Fawzia
Afzal-Khan argues in the context of Pakistan, such convergences often
function to keep women oppressed.[8]

Un-court-ing the Dancing Court: International Female Mobility and the Pull of Domestic Patriarchy

*I entered the Bantul, Yogyakarta, courthouse with an uncertain feel-
ing. It wasn't so much fear, although the fact that I didn't have a
lawyer concerned me to some extent. But I thought, "I know every-
body inside," and I believed my education abroad—and my idealistic
alliance with international feminist praxis—would break the old
stereotype of mistreated women in Third World countries, and the
discourse of agency would help me argue my case and defend myself
in front of the court. Yet the judges are all male. Seven female dancers from Yogyakarta stand at the gate, their gaze uncertain, yet the
presence and position of their bodies expresses their commitment to
incur the risks of engagement. I wait for almost one hour until a court
representative calls my name. The female dance group spontaneously
falls in step behind me, clearly displaying their support. I am seated
by an officer in the defendant's chair; across the room are the seats of
the group representing my accuser. I feel okay. Mostly, I just want to
know what kinds of things they are going to accuse me of, and I am
curious about the language they will use to justify the charges.*

It was the summer of 2002, and I had been forced to take a break from my work in Cambodia to make my appearance in court, where I was obliged to sit and listen to the commands issued me in the steady voice of patriarchy.[9] *I thought back on the past few days before I appeared in this room, when I had danced at the palace of King Norodhom Sihanouk; I remembered exactly where my performance took place, in front of the Buddha, surrounded by a thousand offerings. There, the value of my body was assessed differently, and this was reflected by my movements, mediating the perception of the female dancing body.*

I thought also of my travel on the Japanese boat in Phnom Penh, searching for the myth of the female goddess, the power of Apsara. The sudden transformation from my position as representative of the state—"standing for" it—to a citizen called to appear *before it (both involve rigidly structured court systems) engendered a stark realization: the gap between cultural ambassador and disciplined and unspeaking woman—a dancing body immobilized before the eyes of patriarchal authority—was in this context all but nonexistent.*

Suddenly, the judge raised his hand and declared loudly, "All the women seated behind the defendant should leave this room. This is a closed court." The support of my local alliances was thus momentarily recognized and then quickly made to disappear. The other dancers left the room, and I was alone. Numbly observing the process, I was mesmerized by the darkness of the court's expressions (in the language of legal allegation) and their ability to reconstruct my history, and, moreover, how that reconstructed history seemed able to legitimize whatever decision they were about to make regarding my life and my rights. I listened as my dancing and my travel, despite their seemingly unassailable association with service to the state, were now categorized as "wild behavior." I did not expect such a harsh judgment, such a devaluing of my work, my global education and scholarship reduced to a "failure to perform my female duty" toward men. I was accused of abandoning my filial obligations, leaving a man victimized at home, his life incomplete without an obedient wife. No space was left for me to utter a single word in defense of my desire to travel abroad or to mention my independent earnings or how such a thing could strengthen a household. I heard the gavel knock loudly against the table three times. And the court closed, and all was quiet again.

Two years later, I received a letter from the court, announcing that I was now "released" from my obligations as a wife. In one small way, then, I was free, able to cut certain ties that restrained me, yet at great personal cost. The court did not acknowledge my right to claim any of my belongings that were being held by my ex-husband, and I was thus further unmoored from my sense of belonging in the space of the nation of my birth: I lost most of my dancing costumes, childhood photographs, years of field notes, and even my small home, which I had inherited from my mother.

I read the letter on a flight to the United States, where I hoped to continue my higher education. For me it represented the continuing pull of two different contexts, entangled and affecting each other, in which at one time and place the female dancing body was everything, but at another (and in many ways simultaneously), this significance vanished amid the domestic jurisdiction of men's rights and patriarchal courts. The female dancing body must negotiate each position, residing between idealization and mobility, vilification and punishment.

Since the patriarchal household is embedded in the construction of law, the many travel opportunities available to civil servants in general (many of whom are government bureaucrats) are offered mostly to men, who, upon their return, gain social influence and public leadership status. Meanwhile, women travel mostly in groups, as members of dance troupes or in cultural missions abroad led by a male officer. Here, the two factors controlling women's position are the construction of culture by the nation-state and the conservative Islamic norms that function to limit the level of privilege and true mobility given to (particularly) female performers. Ultimately, this serves to symbolically fix and demystify women through a limited definition of their position as artists or dancers, which then becomes strictly capitalist in terms of their performance of labor. The contemporary manifestation of such structure and limitation demonstrates the strong presence of colonial law within the new Indonesian state, combined with elements of Islamic law (which emerged more recently at the national level during the late New Order period) as adapted by the secular capitalists who developed the nation's constitution. All of these factors contribute to shaping the behavior and experiences of women in ways that often appear paradoxical: the state constitution acknowledges the need for women's emancipation in the process of building a nation, yet the state's regular placement of women in positions that carry mainly symbolic power strategically limits their access to intervene in policymaking.

A similar limitation applies to women who engage in factory and farm work, for whom the position of stay-at-home wife is still enforced as a class-based model. However, in the broader context of contemporary society, such practice has come to be viewed as a failure of economic achievement, driven by the increasingly urgent need to generate more monetary income per household. This ideal specifically applies to women with minimal access to education and class privilege, for whom mobility is usually only possible through migration to neighboring states or the Middle East, where they are most often employed as guest workers: usually maids or servants (in Indonesian the term most often used for export labor is "TKI," *Tenaga Kerja Indonesia*—literally "Labor power from Indonesia—or, more pointedly, "TKW," *Tenaga Kerja Wanita*—"Women's labor power"). Working-class women who try to escape from domestic work or a family farm or business also frequently end up being recruited as sex workers in nearby countries or in the capital city, Jakarta. The construction of policies affecting women with various levels of access and privilege thus appears to play into an ideological system ultimately structured around suppression of dissent and maintenance of the status quo: state development agencies such as the Ministry of Labor encourage women to participate in the workforce yet rely on local agents in small towns and villages who recruit young women without clear guidelines or any promise of protection of their rights or safety.[10] Although a few nongovernmental organizations (NGOs) and UN-sponsored groups have made attempts at fostering more equitable and transparent recruiting in the past ten years, until now they have failed to create a broader narrative of hope for women's empowerment. Yet the discourse of Indonesian nation building continues to declare women equal citizens, encouraging participation in the "free" labor market as a move in the direction of "progress."

Thus, within the state's idealized social construction, the image of the stay-at-home wife is no longer the dominant ideal. However, access to desirable work depends on exclusive education and class-based networks. Sex work, seasonal laboring, and status as a guest worker abroad therefore become the set of limited options for the majority of women. In many regions, centers of prostitution develop with protection from military officers. The policy of exporting women workers to the Middle East also allows abuse and corruption on many state levels, including official recruiters who illegally demand extremely high fees.[11] In some cases women attain managerial positions, but such opportunities are also mostly available to those from upper-class backgrounds with access to elite education. Yet despite their standing, such women must still work under tight social rules. In the case of artists, whatever their backgrounds, they are required by law to obtain the permission of their families in order to practice (thereby limiting their mobility). If they are married (as my appearance in court made very clear), they *must* have the consent of both their husbands and multiple organs of the state[12] for any kind of travel or professional work.

In order to qualify for their (largely) symbolic role in nation building, then, women are expected to be "actual" obedient wives, mothers, and state representatives, their qualifications for which are scrutinized at every level of official and social hierarchy. These normative expectations are often negatively reinforced by images in the media of sexualized females as deviant and threatening, focusing public attention on the power of women's bodies as a potential disturbance of public order, simultaneously masking the violence and injustice that so often befall those same bodies.[13] As discussed in previous chapters, this strategy was deployed during Suharto's rule to control public opinion by demonizing women who actively resisted the state, portraying them as morally debased by the influence of "foreign" progressive values. Popular women's organizations such as Dharma Wanita often embraced such campaigns, allying themselves with the mainstream by supporting the social codes and guidelines defined by male dominance. In this way the military created a systematized fear within those who openly disagreed, or refused to conform with, the state narrative or norm.

As suggested previously, although the performing arts are valued as women's work in many contexts, their esteem is paradoxical; they are also often seen as antagonistic toward expectations of appropriate female behavior, and an ambivalent public attitude toward female dancers prevails. The convergence of these multiple forces of restriction keeps women oppressed on many levels, while their identities and cultural practices are continually sold in local and global markets: as practitioners of dance, women function as an "exhibit" of the illusory, idealized cultural heritage and diversity of Indonesia, one which precisely reveals the prominent position of women within such discourses.

The women who perform abroad are mostly civil servants or young female dancers from the presidential dance troupe SADUPI *(Sarana Duta Perdamaian Indonesia,* Indonesian Representatives for Peace), or private troupes not officially considered organs of the state yet still hosted and led by the head of Dharma Wanita Pusat, the main office of the association of civil servants' wives in Jakarta.[14] Administered by Dharma Wanita, these groups of dancers travel and perform annually, promoting the idea of a nationalized and unified Indonesia. In this context, they cross borders as diplomats, earning—for the women in particular—a certain social leverage and access to upward mobility. In this context, female dancers' intervention and mediation of the significance of cultural practice is made possible, paradoxically, by their aestheticization—via performance and display of "national culture"—and obfuscation of the entire system of control within which they are expected to operate. While the master teachers relied on by the state to train practitioners are often also women, their agency and ability to realize new choreographic forms and ideas are complicated by their embeddedness in a system of exchange that values specifically structured displays of female bodies on stage. Yet as choreographers, and as the majority of the actual bodies that move and perform, women gain the opportunity to create and appear in works that have the potential to be performed outside of spaces subject to strict or direct government control. The corresponding lack of supervision might then enable the temporary inclusion of reflexive or critical elements, such as a less-than-veiled commentary on the problematic sociopolitical context of "Indonesian dance."

The logistics and management of such practice, however, are of course still heavily dependent on the system of control in Indonesia: they require official permits as well as government financial support. So this discursive space, where the female performers and choreographers should be able to produce "resistive choreography," is disrupted yet again by the state's agenda through the distribution of funding *(uang pembinaan)*, which serves to authorize women's choreographic innovation and facilitate development and performance. Thus, the ability to deconstruct the co-optation of women's praxis is severely entangled with its own economic and logistic conditions of possibility. Even so, the situation of the female performance artist is generally viewed as a significant improvement on the condition of most women, simply by virtue of its access to mobility.

Yet as we have seen, more restrictive gender-based conditions are also often selectively applied to women with the status of state cultural practitioners, particularly those who are seen by the government—or family members—as overextending their access to mobility. But despite the thickness of restrictive patriarchal space for all Indonesian women, a few female dancers have been able to find cracks in the walls of control, gradually forming alliances through networking with like-minded artists across the archipelago and through travel abroad.[15] These types of conversations began to emerge more frequently and openly after the fall of Suharto and the institution of *Reformasi* in 1998, which at least ushered in a greater sense of hope for the relaxation of Indonesian state control over the arts and thereby engendered something like a tentative boldness in practitioners. In this context, artists have the potential ability to use mobile, global performance spaces (as well as localized ones) to examine the existing channels of power and explore the possible resources of resistance to state domination and the various, resultant abuses of human rights, beginning, perhaps, with domestic issues faced by women.

An example of one such group is *Sahita,* a troupe of female dancers from Central Java that use a local language (Javanese) to create spoken and sung narration for their choreography, which critiques the fabric and practices of everyday life. Often strategically deploying humor to examine issues of power and leadership in local matters, their performances have focused on questions such as the maintenance of men's traditional role as head of the household within contemporary village economies where both housework and financial stability often come from women (frequently through selling vegetables in the market). In the context of *Sahita*'s public representations, "heads of the household" are sometimes portrayed as parasites, whose main contribution is to sit around, give orders, and roll cigarettes for themselves. The result of pointed revelations regarding the potential ridiculousness of men's ubiquitous authority is a symbolic attack bolstered by the public participation of the audience through heckling and laughter.

Mirroring the context of *Sahita* on a larger scale, for state dancers attempts at resistance are also most plausible at a safe remove from the imposed national center (village dancers stay "outside" to avoid its gaze, while state dancers move even further out, attempting to leave national space itself behind). When the female dancer is in a diasporic location or position, she is able to perform or choreograph outside of the sphere of direct state influence. (Here I point out that the attenuation of fear is often due to the perception—however illusory—of protection through entrance into the academic world.) However, in many cases, the demand in Western countries is for beautified and exoticized cultural expressions, often based on ideals that have been established and proffered by the governments of non-Western states (after being developed in the context of colonial or imperial world relations). Thus, embodied, resistant or experimental commentaries on sociopolitical context still face a daunting array of obstacles in order to gain acceptance in the realm of world dance and the global stage.

Women's Citizenship: The Dance of Leaving Home

Jakarta, 2001. My confrontation with the local court of law still ahead of me, I was on my way to Los Angeles, beginning a highly anticipated journey that would involve postponing my professional obligations at home, where I was a civil servant and professor of dance; this was considered a very good position in a country that was still struggling with its identity as a democratic state and trying to figure out what to do with, among other things, a long-standing surplus of women's labor.

Leaving despite strong objections at the level of the local institution where I taught, I had no expectations of a send-off celebration. With an outside grant and a somewhat shaky travel permit from a higher level of administration, I entered the Jakarta airport alone. Perhaps not surprisingly, it was full of women: workers getting ready to leave for Dubai, the Middle East, Hong Kong, and Singapore, crossing borders in response to the call of the extensive foreign market for domestic female labor.

Nearby, hundreds of women stood in a long line waiting to be checked in, easily identifiable by their cheap, matching headscarves, which were blue in color and jilbab style (constructed of tight, elastic material with a built-in, hatlike brim above the face). These women, however, were responding to the call of a different market, one based on spiritual value, whose center of exchange was also located abroad. To get there, they would cross borders temporarily by way of cheap, package tours bound for Mecca, the birthplace of the prophet and idealized holy land, bringing home a sense of greater piousness and the possibility of increased social (and thereby also economic) status in the context of Indonesian Islam.

Following a similar, yet visibly lower-status dress code—with a forcibly synchronized polyester material for their headscarves and the same color pants, shoes, and bags—several other groups of women were walking in the rigidly organized lines typical of guest workers or TKW. I walked along beside the first group but used a separate entrance at the boarding gate; as I glanced over, I was met with frightened gazes from some of the women, especially those who appeared to be very young. Their eyes wandered timidly between the Indonesian immigration officer and the local "third man": the broker or agent for female domestic labor abroad. In many ways the most powerful figures in these transactions, the authority and legal operating status of such third men are usually left unquestioned by women and officials alike, both of whom must rely on them for access to surplus capital.

The absence of celebration or ceremony in these women's departure perhaps marks the nervousness of higher government offices regarding the movement of women and labor outside of the regular mechanisms of government control. Despite having in many ways simply "let go" of these women, the state nonetheless attempts to keep up the appearance of responsibility for its own citizens. The plight of female workers abroad often triggers criticism from the international community, where Indonesia is already categorized by the World Bank and other institutions as a poor country with a high rate of displacement.

At the next gate, another group of female Islamic pilgrims is gathered; despite the similarity of their "uniforms" to those of the guest workers, in this Mecca-bound party a sense of community is more clearly visible. Things seem hectic yet less tense, and there are many happy faces of family members accompanying them on their departure for the holy land. This group of (mostly) women are preparing their trip to Mecca according to a special category of pilgrimage known as umroh. *In Indonesia,* umroh, *or "haj-light" as it is sometimes known, has become the clearest example of the intersection between the economy of religion and women's faith. The trip is quite expensive, and thousands of dollars have changed hands in order for each of these women to visit—in relative comfort—the land upon which the Prophet Mohammad once walked. Logistical matters for such tours are based on level of expenditure, which determines the level of hotel (standard, deluxe, and so on) as well as its proximity to the main, designated mosque for daily prayers (rooms with air conditioning that do not require a lengthy walk under the extremely hot sun are often in short supply). Like membership in an airline frequent flyer program, privilege and service follow brand loyalty.*

Unlike the other women workers or myself, those leaving on umroh *have likely received a joyous sendoff. Often an entire family, or even a whole village in several cars or buses will escort the women until they enter the airport. In such cases, the celebration signifies the gain in social status received by an entire community via the pilgrims from among their own ranks.*

Watching the various Indonesian women who would cross borders on the same day as myself, I felt somehow lucky to have come alone, without guides, friends or chaperones, or anyone who might

*seek symbolic or material profit from their attachment to my trip. My
movement in many ways was motivated by detachment, an attempt
to free myself from the strictures of performance and official behavior
that had come to dominate my life, so that I might attempt to stand
outside for a moment and gaze in. Yet I would never be completely
outside my home or my place of birth, or, as I increasingly came to
realize, out of reach of the state for which I had served as representative. But moving down the concourse, I did begin to feel a new sense
of control over my body, as if, at least for the moment, I had become a signifier of my own possibilities for escape and independence.
(This feeling, of course, discounted the fact of my presence within the
highly capitalized, global space of an international airport.)*

*The feeling lasted as far as Singapore: just as I reached the
gate for my transit to the United States, it closed in front of me,
and I was informed that all flights to the United States were can-
celled. No exceptions. My moving physical form, it seemed, had
been quickly reattached to its "state of origin" and was being held
until further notice. It was September 11, 2001, and because my
passport identified me as Muslim by association (Indonesia is, of
course, the "world's largest Muslim nation"), I waited for two
weeks before I was given a permit that classified me as an "unthreatening body." At this divisive time in history, the sudden
reimagining of borders served to create and recreate a discourse of
alliances, revealing a pointed international coalition defined by its
shifting, collective judgments of the character of certain nation states
according to new criteria.*

*Finally, however, my plane took off, and I was on my way
to the jungle of Western higher education; after landing safely in
Los Angeles, I was faced with the fear and uncertainty of still
another vexed border crossing. Yet I have trained myself to keep
defining and redefining possibilities, acknowledging that going
and coming requires a certain (at times very certain) surrender of
dignity. As a "diaspora subject" and a "postcolony object," I have
always had to reconfigure my location and its position within national and global structures. Thus, as a response, I turn to something of a meta-ethnography of coming and going—a discourse on
women with borders, the real and the imaginary, immigration and*

belonging—attempting to categorize, redefine, and objectify my
multiple, conflicting alliances from the theoretical standpoint of a
(transplanted) scholar at a Western university.

Aihwa Ong promotes the idea of "flexible citizenship," which
refers to the patriarchal world of Hong Kong's business class, pointing to the specific mobility of citizens who gain access to the mechanisms of capitalist production. By examining the business class in
particular in relation to the broader contexts surrounding it, Ong
argues that its members not only conceptualize and create the new
nation-state but also construct the state (in this instance a city-state,
Hong Kong) in a manner that serves the perpetuation of the global
economy.[16]

In my work, "flexible citizenship" is used in reference to Indonesian women who practice performing arts, are employed by the
government, and often travel abroad. *Flexible* in this discussion refers
to state-sanctioned female performers in comparison to other female citizens who have minimal opportunity to negotiate the ways
in which their citizenship materializes. However, conditions are
flexible for these women only insofar as they continue to appear as if
they were serving the interests of the Indonesian state and patriarchal
society: to some degree their labor must function to promote the
circulation of certain values. Travel by women performers abroad
is viewed as an honor and as a legitimate means to gain respect and
earn a good wage. Yet women return to a very fragile position in
society, where their every move is scrutinized methodically in an effort to restrain their new corporeal flexibility from overflowing the
boundaries set for it by the patriarchal state.

The performing arts, particularly dance, must by definition be
flexible to a certain degree, as they represent multiple elements considered necessary in order for Indonesia to look and function properly as a nation—national treasure, commodity for export, symbol of
the state, symbol of refinement in court cultural practice, and sacred
ritual—all of which, when kept within specifically defined degrees
of movement and meaning, serve to foster historical amnesia within
the country, as well as frequently encouraging misguided conceptions of multiculturalism and Western Orientalism from without.

Therefore, as I have argued in this book, I must acknowledge that in this process, the possibility of negotiation for women artists is regimented by their "glocal" national and international practice, the intended function of which is mimetic replication of the bodies, techniques, and symbolic power of vanished, banned, or murdered artists. Yet I have also argued that this "performing" is a practice that opens a possible discursive and emotional space for women's participation in the reconfiguration of female citizenship.

Since dance training and performance have become part of the national educational curriculum, more women have been eligible to gain access to higher education. Here we can see the potential reconfiguration of the co-optation enacted by state mandates, both domestically and in relation to the global market, through the mediation of citizenship. Women, through their necessary mobility and partial ownership of the fluid space of performance and expression constructed from their bodily experience and practice, at some level always intervene in the cultural construction of the Indonesian nation-state.

More recently, female performers employed by the state have been viewed as pioneers by certain feminist scholars, as artists creating alternative spaces for women's voices even as they continue by necessity to negotiate with their patriarchal patronage.[17] Given that everyday decision making requires women to straddle the line between greater freedom of expression and acquiescing to expected behavior, as I have seen in my ethnographic research, many female artists are particularly aware of how patriarchal domination functions. Therefore, members of the community of female performance artists can serve as powerful, creative sources of knowledge and experience to highlight the role of women and analyze its possibilities as a resource on which the patriarchal nation-state and global economy depend. The potential to resist comes precisely through a better understanding of the fluidity of women's position within the overall structure, which enables negotiation of their participation in systems of representation that oppress them, both at home and abroad.

A more detailed look at dance in the Indonesian academic context reveals that many female performing artists are able to experiment with contemporary approaches to traditional dance within the local, by modifying existing themes as well as creating their own spaces for the placement, manipulation, and display of popular cultural codes. However, such national-level experimentation is, for the most part, still limited by the availability of funding from foreign institutions, or, in rare instances, from the Indonesian Ministry of Culture, Ministry of Tourism, or universities' designated budgets for special events under the banner of *lomba Tari Kontemporer* (contemporary dance competition). In the context of the widespread cultural perspective established by the state and the institutions of world dance, the major obstacles in developing and presenting new forms of expression stem from the perception that any work that is not a replication of established tradition will challenge both established traditions and entrenched policies and social norms. Thus, works that seek to seriously engage their own conditions of possibility—the politics of culture and history in which they are necessarily immersed—may be difficult for an international audience to accept, or to grasp, and may even be rejected at home, where audiences sometimes "know" their own national culture all too well and critique those who are seen as modifying or appending traditional practice.

Nonetheless, certain local artists, despite their immersion—in some cases, from "birth"[18]—in the Indonesian national grid of arts and education, have shown themselves difficult to fully contain within its structure. For such artists, a mastered, official technique, particularly *because* of its strict guidelines, may serve, in subtle or not so subtle ways, to reveal the forces of history and embodied memory churning beneath its surface, as both the "timeless" beauty of the form and the incredible restraint it places on movement become simultaneously visible. Thus, a potential space of resistance is in some sense created every time a practitioner embodies, and subtly modifies, a known form. Yet it is up to the practitioner, as well as the audience—both through active display and by looking, reading, and analyzing movements and variations—to foreground and make visible this excess: that which is not fully suppressed or contained by the nationalized technique. It is through such a combination of display and pointed *reading,* perhaps, that it becomes possible to begin to work within the system to expand the limitations it places on women's mobility and agency. In a sense, this process involves unlocking the potential contained in certain forms by reading—and, to some extent, performing—national culture "against the grain." The forms may thus be slowly imbued with increasing numbers of pointed variations: small changes that symptomatically "speak" of details of experience while continuing to be recognizable as Indonesian and simultaneously (re)rendering what is known as Indonesian dance as alive: containing fluidity and growth.

Globalizing "Movement" and Extreme Stillness: Place/Space and Discontinuity

The travel of women from the postcolony provides a tool to analyze the ways in which the citizenship of the female body itself becomes a seduction, giving me the "intellectual nerve"—the confidence to stand in judgment, to analyze, to see the connections among dance practices, the nation-states' agendas, and the theorization of agency and mobility and their imbrication in globalization. Travel and movement, which are often viewed by global feminism as a sign of the onset of modernity and agency, in a cultural sense, are of course *not* something new that began only with the so-called postmodern approach: in this case, that of idealized sublation of the Other within the timeless imagery of multiculturalist hyperreality. The discourse of mobility is something that exists not only within the sphere of Western academia, but in this narrative of women and dancing transmitted through various local systems of knowledge. In the context of Java it is traditionally known as *Mbarang Neng Sabrang*. *Mbarang Neng Sabrang* is a proverb in Javanese about the crossing of borders. *Mbarang* is traveling and performing; *Neng:* at, on, or in; *Sabrang:* across the border, outside your own home or village, or across the water, river, or ocean. The discourse of *Sabrang* in Javanese, of course, also changes with respect to historical circumstance and to its destination and geographic point of origin. Thus, it has more recently been applied to the travels—whether in the context of performing "culture" or domestic labor—of Indonesian women outside of national space.

Sabrang has come to mean crossing the ocean or border (that is, going abroad). This changing geographic reference also indicates a different type of work or level of income, such as in the case of women guest workers abroad; their *Sabrang* is to the Middle East, Hong Kong, Singapore, Malaysia, or Taiwan. They are not performing anymore in the sense of traditional aesthetics (with its connotations—however unstable—of a certain level of status or respect), but rather providing domestic labor. This is a specific form of travel that interweaves the processes of embodiment (as opposed, here, to more conscious "performance") of an economically based cultural identity and border crossing, the results of which illusively promise a higher income, and, potentially, class status. As always, in Java, the narrative of travel—the myth of access and mobility in *Mbarang Neng Sabrang*—spreads itself contagiously, a paradigm of voluntary displacement that promises mobility and escape yet places you in the ambiguous position of cooptation and resistance, sublimation and surrender.

Following Aihwa Ong,[19] for performing artists in particular, the myth of *Mbarang Neng Sabrang* may be compared to the contemporary concept of the free-trade zone within the global economy. In economic terms, the free-trade zone is a space for localized production in the Third World where there are natural resources, labor, and duty-free products as well as barrier-free trade. In my analysis, traveling female performers are both co-opted labor and active agents within the free-trade zone of the global stage, where mobile cultural labor is imported and positioned at points of intersection within transnational networks of power and trade.[20] While those who work in literal free-trade contexts are often solely valued for their physical labor materialized as products with exchange value, artists are valued not only for their physical labor but also for their cultural knowledge, which aesthetically transforms the moving, gesturing bodies onstage into a recognizable, cohesive product to be consumed in the marketplace of global politics and imperial desire. Yet despite their slightly more flexible citizenship and leverage based on cultural skills, how are artists to "capitalize," in any significant way, on the purported freedom of the special regions in which they perform? Is it possible, climbing the ladders of civil service, or even escaping to the international realm of Western academia, to find oneself in a "trade-free zone" of political engagement and real activism? Or do we find ourselves in an eternal space for the production of ever more apparently convincing theories?

In *Critical Moves: Dance Studies in Theory and Politics,* Randy Martin expands the notion of movement to include the concept of "mobilization," emphasizing that political theory must include attention to the active participation of citizens. To make the connection between dance practices and political economy in everyday life, Martin suggests that dance will help develop fluency in the language of mobilization of power: not a dominant or alien power visited on the body, but what the body can accomplish through movement. Dance assembles movement and reflects the body's capacity to reposition and change, in essence, calling attention to its apparently unique flexibility and the potential contained therein. This convergence is mobilized through the creation of a product, the resulting technique or part thereof, and through the process of production. For Martin, the product is not the aesthetic or ideological effect of the dance, but the materialized *identity* realized through performance.[21]

In this context, I agree that it is important to see the connections between the core principles of dance movement and the role—through varying degrees of its presence or absence—of movement in political practice. I also value the connections Martin makes between the political landscape and the body, as well as his examination of how dance relates to the question of mobilizing bodies within a resistive project of moving, or the movements of postcolonial bodies.

Yet finally, in my own work, after all the various kinds of movement it has entailed, I find myself suddenly back where I started—or in a strikingly similar place—as if I had come full circle and begun unconsciously retracing my steps. From "here," then, I propose that if we see a connection between movement in dance and mobilization, in the case of postcolonial bodies from places like Indonesia, we must also consider the *stillness* that is prevalent in most Southeast Asian court dance practices. These forms of expression, which dominate nationalist cultural production in countries like Indonesia and Cambodia, require the absence of movement, along with the unseen continuation of breathing as rhythm. While there is a significant amount of near-motionlessness, these techniques are still considered to be crucial elements of "dance." Given Martin's point of view, how would this approach to positionality and change—or even to the concept of motion as constitutive of development—relate to participation in the political economy of movements? How do we define *stillness*? Here I return to the importance of reading and the production and reception of "excessive" meaning in the subtle modification of technique, or perhaps even within a rote duplication of form so strictly adherent to "tradition" that it exceeds normative expectations and calls attention to itself.

In the case of Indonesia, and particularly in its nationalized sublimation of the arts of the Javanese court as an imposed stand-in for all other local forms and their practitioners, the "extreme" stillness of dance can be read as containing the unseen. In this context, it must necessarily function to recall, to call up or conjure, the convergence of a powerful form, its former masters, and the unthinkable events of history, foregrounding the very closeness of death that the dance, as embodied by new performers, is officially meant to conceal. The excess is thus precisely conveyed by the lack of motion, by the fact of both actively dancing and, for long stretches of time, remaining completely immobile, as if imitating the impossible reification of culture or the stillness of a real body whose soul has been removed, passed away permanently from the concerns of culture, citizenship, or political activism (although this is perhaps where the latter's "spirit" could be said to live on).

The First Return: Desiring the Archive

The body is lying down, her eyes closed and in full dress. She is inside the keranda, *a Javanese Muslim-style casket used to carry corpses from home to place of burial. She has the long hair, black, white, and red clothing, and special accessories of a* Gandrung[22] *dancer. Her hat is decorated with a sharp needle, an instrument rumored, under adverse circumstances, to have been deployed as a poison-tipped weapon, swung unexpectedly into the soft skin of a male partner's face with a deft, circular movement of the dancer's body. Here it is placed directly above the woman's earring, sharply standing out even as her head lies motionless on the pillow, as if warning anyone who might deign to disturb her silent repose. She is lying down in full costume, symbolizing death, and the forgotten deaths of those whose glamour once matched hers.*

The scene takes place in Yogyakarta, Java, just outside the palace walls and within close reach of the national Institute of the Arts. The woman in the casket is part of a museum-like display through which the audience must walk to reach the seating area for the performance. I purposely cast a dancer who is famous in the city, hoping to create moments of discomfort when the audience enters the lobby. The spectators, lined up outside, are allowed to enter the space one by one or in small groups. They do so in a careful way, stepping quietly. Hidden in the back, I try to observe the effects of the scenery on their bodily response, as they wander without explicit guidance through the "postmodern" space preceding the stage. Some show a readiness to enter the more structured space of performance to come, yet many display a disciplined attention, seeming to realize that they, too, are a crucial part of this exhibition.

With no explicit boundaries between spectators and performers, the audience moves through slowly, seemingly trying to engage with the human objects on display. Some of them laugh, while others seem a bit frightened. Interestingly, others attempt to open conversations with the familiar bodies of the "dead."

The coffin and the prostrate body in particular, easily recognizable to most of Yogyakarta's prominent arts community, receive a lot of attention. Certain audience members, in fact, approaching the coffin, stop to remind the artist to be aware of the risks she undertakes: in Java it is very taboo to choreograph images of death on stage, or to invoke or play with death in relation to the particularities of history, displaying it visibly on stage or in a public space. But I planned this—to open this evening's performance with the casket as an aesthetic historiography of death, to bring them face to face with the taboo. I want to express my everyday feelings of confrontation with authorities and various colleagues alike, by speaking through the socionormative code of taboo in the presentation of memory in this display.

As Jean Luc Nancy suggests in his chronicle of consecration and massacre, "The everyday then takes charge, simultaneously, of the repetition of the shock and its erasure."[23] *Here, I wanted to adapt Nancy's ideas of erasure, to suggest that the everyday visibil-*

ity of the arts in Indonesia can be read as containing the marginal
values of what should (not) be known. In order to comment on that
condition, I attempt to create a shock by emphasizing the taboo in
the everyday stillness of elements of culture and art. I try to take
the choreography of nationalized dance and dancing bodies into the
realm of experimental methodology, to create a moment of interpre-
tation, of connection in relation to the other bodies that have dis-
appeared and are no longer able to get up and move and be applauded
after the show. I hope to bring to the stage at least the recognition of
death within the familiar and the everyday: movements, techniques,
and bodies that are otherwise a source of joy and pride in tradition.

That night, the opening of *Tembok Mari Bicara* (Talk to the Wall)
on August 21, 2008, the "museum" was housed in the lobby of the
French Cultural Center in Yogyakarta, a zone of mostly French and
local art and performance in which we somehow felt safer to put on
this highly politicized, if still somewhat coded, work; while the space
caters to local, mostly Indonesian and Javanese audiences—those who
are implicated in, and thus have the best chance of "reading" our domestic critique—any attack or attempt by local authorities to censor
would necessarily have to be carefully considered in relation not only
to domestic policies but to the sphere of Indonesia's international relations. The decision to put on the show was still a gamble, both for
ourselves and for the young French director of the center, who herself (as opposed to the institution of the center) wields little political
clout in either France or Java. Our calculations, however, appeared
sound: a one-night-only performance in a small, 200 person venue
would not likely be seen as worth the risk of negative publicity if it
were shut down. Nonetheless, the promotion and publicity materials
were evasive, mentioning nothing about the massacres or the specific
politics of the show. This may also have been a factor in the lack of
reticence among many of the pillars of Yogyakarta's established arts
community—those whom the work was in many ways aimed at—to
come and see, or read, what we were up to. I was surprised at the
strength of response: the space quickly filled to capacity, and many
latecomers were unable to enter.

From the performance of Tembok Mari Bicara, French Cultural Center, Yogyakarta, Java: Young village dancers turned soldiers (from the staged dance performance, not the "museum" section). Dancers: Novi, Nila, Unung, Desia. Photographer/copyright: Rachmi Diyah Larasati.

The conception and realization of this particular event would perhaps have been inconceivable without my long periods of residence and study outside of Indonesia (including the basic factor of access to funding allocatable to experimental, politically oriented work here). Yet I believed that it also represented, and was embedded in, a slowly growing trend among locally based artists to address some of the most thorny, risky issues at home: matters whose source is directly underfoot every time we step onto a domestic stage. Thus, in planning, producing, and carrying out *Tembok Mari Bicara,* I was neither alone nor unable to share and discuss the project within the local arts community, although I was certainly cautious in hiring dancers and members of the crew.

My main collaborator, Setyastuti, is a well-known choreographer, dancer, and colleague from the Yogyakarta Institute of the Arts (ISI) and is known as a prominent Muslim artist in the context of Java. I have counted Setyastuti as one of my closest, and most open-minded, friends since our days as young professors of dance at ISI

in the early 1990s. Yet perhaps because of her strong, inherited attachment to both the palace and the local arts administration, our
first conversation about the possibility of creating something more
explicitly critical together—and with it a necessary discussion of
my own history and complex, genealogical-political identity—took
place only after more than a decade of friendship, in 2004. She, too,
is a female civil servant, in her case a particularly "clean" one who
grew up surrounded by government officers and royalty, beginning
her career as a dancer in the palace when she was very young. Yet
it was not only her later, famous proclivity for modernist technical experimentation that bolstered my courage to open up to her: it
was precisely the way she embodied and interpreted the stillness of
the court technique that finally—having seen and studied her highly
regarded performances since long before I made her acquaintance—
sparked the recognition of a potential kindred spirit.

For Setyastuti, however, rather than the extended, "deathlike"
immobility displayed by other dancers, the clue was her inability,

Jailangkung, experimental choreography based on a Javanese children's game
involving "spirit possession," by Setyastuti in collaboration with Koes Yuliadi and
Warsana Kliwir, colleagues from the Institute of the Arts, Yogyakarta. Minneapolis,
2010. Photographer: Fiza Jaafar-Tribbet. Copyright: Rachmi Diyah Larasati.

Setyastuti performs in Perempuan dan Islam: Terbangan (Women and Islam: *Terbangan*), choreographed by Setyastuti and Diyah Larasati, Surakarta, Central Java, July 2010. Photographer: Piping Da Costa. Copyright: Rachmi Diyah Larasati.

or unwillingness, to keep her body absolutely still, despite decades of training in the highest institution of Javanese culture. While her expression and the pose of her head and limbs were the picture of formal perfection, the middle fingers of her outstretched hand—which was itself held, true to form, at an impossibly obtuse angle to her arm—betrayed the tiny signs of restlessness, moving apart and then together again as if in time to some unseen rhythm pulsing from within. It was here, watching a seemingly endless—yet always strangely fascinating—repetition of the most official and sublimated of dances, that I first began to read, and to feel, the presence of that which "exceeds," if only slightly, even the most hegemonic and deterministic of embodied national representations.

The third major collaborator in our performance, the music composer Y. Subowo, is also a high level civil servant who, like Setyastuti and myself, has worked on many Indonesian state cultural missions. In his case, we were brought together as collaborators by his literal, historical experience of stillness: the presence of hundreds of bodies buried only inches beneath the sand of a riverbed in the middle of the village that was his childhood home. Because of the un-erasable memories of his youth in the mid-1960s, his alliance with the state, which, like Setyastuti's and my own, has enabled a career filled with travel and artistry and has been tempered by the lingering questions that come with the witnessing of a mass crime. Nonetheless, for both of my collaborators and myself, this project has been risky; it constitutes a big step in the negotiation of our various professional, social, and political attachments and alliances. The process began slowly, with a long conversation ending in a workshop in 2004; here I first proposed a set of more concrete political themes, which, in our intermittent conversations tempered by the separate meditations of each of us, led to the commitment to produce *Tembok Mari Bicara* in 2008.

The artistic, political space opened by our collaboration, and the geographically local, yet international place created by the presence of the French Cultural Center, are of course not the constitutive elements of an idealized "trade-free zone" of pure expression. Perhaps closer to a temporary space for the suspension of certain imposed duties, nonetheless the exchange that took place there involved a great

Y. Subowo performs in "Earth Day: *Mempertanyakan Kebersihan Air* (Questioning the Purity of Water)." Yogyakarta, Java, 2010. Photographer: Rini. Collection of Y. Subowo. Copyright: Y. Subowo.

number of connections and assumed "debts" to the various national bodies involved, particularly that of Indonesia. Yet in light of the relative success of our event, and the increasing numbers of openly politically "subversive" Indonesians in which I view our work as embedded (like those who put on the 2005 event commemorating the forty-year anniversary of the killings in 1965),[24] I am hopeful that we are, in fact, taking steps in the direction of greater public openness to the facts of our personal and collective histories.

She dresses in sampot, *as the dancers on the* Amiral-Kersaint *are described when they arrived in France. But unlike that time, her dance will be performed in the palace of King Sihanouk. The facial expression of the dancer in this performance is very serious— reported on and recorded by a variety of machines. In the palace of Sihanouk, she has been asked to perform a Cambodian dance for a presentation to be sent to UNESCO, specifically in order to show how foreigners from neighboring countries have been attracted to this cultural heritage of Cambodia. This is a candidacy process, through which UNESCO decides which country and arts group will receive*

TARI KONTEMPORER

𝕿𝖊𝖒𝖇𝖔𝖐: 𝕸𝖆𝖗𝖎 𝕭𝖎𝖈𝖆𝖗𝖆!

KAMIS
21
AGUSTUS
2008

19.30 WIB

LIP
AUDITORIUM
(JALAN SAGAN 3)

KOREOGRAFER:
SETYASTUTI & DIYAH LARASATI
PENATA ARTISTIK:
DIYAH LARASATI & SETYASTUTI
PENATA MUSIK:
Y. SUBOWO
STAGE/LIGHTING:
VERY & GROUP
PENARI:
NOVIAN OCTASARI
HARIN
ELIZABET NILA
DOZI
NUR AINI
DIAN
YESI IKAYANI
DIYAH LARASATI
UTI SEYASTUTI
SEKAR
BEKTI BUDI HASTUTI
RAHMIDA
MUSISI
IMUNG
DENY
NOVI
SANDYO
SUNYOTO
PUTRI
Y. SUBOWO

Promotional poster for Tembok Mari Bicara, 2008. Copyright: Rachmi
Diyah Larasati.

an award. At issue are copyright and ownership, the capitalization
of dance technique. The occasion provides her a significant encounter with the Cambodian dance scene, the space of cultural heritage
and source of aesthetic essentialism. It seems to her the event serves
to canonize the work of Auguste Rodin with the dancers of the

Amiral-Kersaint. *There, in the late nineteenth century, his Euro-*
pean mechanism of interpretation and fascination produced draw-
ings of Cambodian dancing legs. The European encounter, now,
through the postmodern approach to cultural distance, is being re-
placed by the UNESCO award ceremony.

Here, in the midst of another transnational, multiply co-opted
artistic "free-trade zone" in 2002, is where I locate a postscript, one
of the various "ends" of this book. This work is embedded in the
economy of the Western academy—in this case the financial network
behind my career that necessitates the creation of a book: as product,
symbol of achievement, and, I believe, as a sincere expression of political critique that I am grateful to have had the opportunity to create. As such, this book would not have been possible without my use
of the most globalized, sublimated technique currently in existence:
the English language, the mandatory, standard global form because
of its relative universality, if not egalitarianism. Thus, while I have
already made arrangements for an Indonesian translation, the book
you are reading will necessarily be the "first."

In a similar vein, then, I frame Indonesian history in more universalized terms by comparison to the widely known Southeast Asian
case of Cambodia. However, the (reconstructed) Cambodian code in
approaching the ideal conception of body and, of course, the specifics
of Cambodian history, are different. The dance is a choreographed
replication of the gestures of temple statues, freezing the alignment
of the body even when it moves to the side: the upper body does
not serve as an anchor point from which the head and legs move
separately, thus it creates a far straighter line than its counterpart in
the Javanese court. In Cambodia, the memories of the time of the
Khmer Rouge are directly, publicly linked to the killing of dancers,
artists, and millions of others that occurred in the attempt to reshape
an entire culture under the unrelenting fist of Pol Pot. Cambodian
court dance, too, while at times unsustainably held up as an ideal
of opposition and resistance to the history of terror, is nonetheless
able to be connected, as if by a straight line, to the stillness of death
lying beneath it. Likewise, in the eyes of the international community, the application of the term *genocide* to certain historical events

in Cambodia produces a straight line that leads from the global acknowledgment of politicized mass murder to a universal conception of wrongdoing and evil.

While I do not seek to blur the myriad, constitutive distinctions between Cambodian and Javanese or Indonesian experiences of history, nor to overly exploit the basic similarities of our nationalized cultures, I suggest that it is high time for the international community to cease being diverted by the "indirection" of Javanese court dance and Indonesian artistic performance—normally represented and understood as a symbolic detour from the knowledge of mass murder in the archipelago—and to connect the facts of history with the "universal" language of horror. In the use of the term *genocide,* Robert Gelattely and Ben Kiernan suggest that the UN convention of 1948 requires the proven intent of perpetrators to exterminate an entire community: "the intent to destroy, in whole, part, a national, ethnical, racial or religious group, as such."[25] As Gelattely and Kiernan further elaborate, within international law, genocide describes deliberate mass extermination campaigns specifically motivated by fear or hatred of a victim group, yet a group specifically defined in political terms should not be included. In Indonesia, in the context of the international community where the mass killings under Suharto have only recently been acknowledged, the consensus is that there were massacres in 1965–66, but no "genocide" has ever occurred except in the more recent case of mass killings in East Timor in the late 1970s, which targeted an ethnically defined, and mostly Catholic, group.[26]

However, in this book, I use *genocide* to refer to the politically motivated massacres in Indonesia during the rise of Suharto, where those being targeted were presented as a threatening political group (communist, PKI) as well as a religious one: claims, for the most part unfounded, of the atheism of PKI members were used to inflame and turn other citizens against them on religious grounds, particularly in the specifically Islamic context of East Java.[27] In terms of the minimum of hundreds of thousands of citizens who lost their lives, it is obvious that no such clearly defined grouping of victims can actually be claimed to have existed prior to the killings. This is further complicated by the subsequent *dis*claiming (in many cases truthfully) of any political affiliation with communism by many of the relatives of those killed, or by those who escaped death but were imprisoned for alleged involvement with the left. Yet despite the somewhat unclear or fabricated guidelines used to define and target the massive group whose lives were taken by Suharto and the military, by the acts themselves and by the ways in which they were carried out, the victims were indeed forcibly "unified" and aligned as a collective entity by their attackers. Certainly, during the period from late 1965 to early 1966, suspected members of the PKI were treated as specific, and different, "kinds" of persons than other Indonesian citizens, and thus they were targeted "for destruction on the basis of what are presumed to be more or less inherited, perhaps genetic, shared group characteristics that the victims cannot divest nor be reasonably expected to divest, irrespective of their intentions or actions."[28] Ethnic Chinese Indonesians were also disproportionately pursued by the military because of suspected ties to communist China. After the bulk of the killings had ceased, the continued targeting of even distant relatives of those killed or arrested also produced a strong genealogic aspect to the new political underclass of the Suharto years. Thus it would appear, in the face of the overwhelming evidence of what happened, who was responsible, and what the motivating factors were, that the international community led by Europe and the United States must follow its own policies for the classification of the mass murders by Suharto and the military in the case of Indonesia. They must again draw a straight line of condemnation between such historical actions and a universally understood evil, despite their own unflagging support of the leading perpetrators at the time when the genocide occurred.

NOTES

Introduction

1. The dances I am talking about here are those that were not taught at my school. Mostly the movements follow the improvised gestures of the leader (often imitating women walking as if in slow motion), along with the singing of other women (usually about the moon, or *rembulan* in Javanese). The dancers gradually form a circle or long line.

2. "Clean environment" or *Bersih Lingkungan* is a special term to determine genealogical political roots within family trees. In 1968–98 this term was most often used to screen citizens' eligibility to work in public service, military, as a state employee, or in the private sector. Many Javanese and Balinese families used "clean environment" as a moral code to judge their family members' spousal choices.

3. However, many traces of a greater male presence would insistently appear at the house, marked by the thick, large-scale wooden *wayang kayu* puppets, *keprak* (a small wooden box that the puppet master strikes to accent action and mark time), and *blangkon* (a traditional Javanese man's hat) and completed with an empty birdhouse of refined, teak construction and a few sickles for working the fields. These traces, captured in memory, of other male figures who had once inhabited or been attached to the house did not correspond with Mr. Soek's own signifying presence.

4. Although many women in villages were not members of Gerwani, the obvious alliances created through a shared experience of womanhood and women's issues often served to mark the link between the relatively uneducated women in villages and their wealthier, formally schooled counterparts

who were official members of Gerwani. The "evidence" of involvement in public discussions of things like women's changing roles in the workplace was more than enough for many nonmembers to be suspected and arrested by authorities.

5. Edward Said, *The World, the Text, and the Critic* (Cambridge, Mass.: Harvard University Press, 1983), 1–31.

6. While I was of course aware of the disappearances in my family and those around me, my work with certain professors at UCLA in particular provided a broader, more "empirical" understanding of the events surrounding them, and the sense of a fragmented global community that was, if at times somewhat un-self-reflexively, keeping track of such things and attempting to hold regimes accountable by drawing international attention to them. Many reports archived in the Cornell library (rare manuscript section) were also extremely helpful in mapping both the general political landscape of Indonesia around 1965, and the connections between certain U.S. academics, government officers, and, in fact, artists and dancers, and the violent, anti-leftist rise of Suharto during the height of the Cold War.

7. I refer to the translation of the P4 course description in Joseph Saunders, *Academic Freedom in Indonesia: Dismantling Soeharto-Era Barriers* (New York: Human Rights Watch, 1998), 62.

1. To Remember Differently

1. See Richard Schechner, "Wayang Kulit in the Colonial Margin," *Drama Review* 34, no. 2 (Summer 1990): 25–67; Felicia Hughes Freeland, "A Throne for the People: Observation of the Jumenengan Sultan Hamengkubuwono X," *Indonesia,* no. 51 (April 1991): 129–52; Mohd. Anis Md Noor, "Kapila Vatsyayan and Dance Scholarship: India and Beyond," *Dance Research Journal* 32, no. 1 (Summer 2000): 95–102.

2. For a detailed analysis of dance and performing arts as historical mediators between Indonesia and other (particularly European) nations, see Matthew Isaac Cohen, *Performing Otherness: Java and Bali in International Stages 1905–1953* (New York: Palgrave, 2010). Cohen profoundly demonstrates how the image of Java and Balinese dance migrated to Europe and the United States even before the arrival of Indonesian dancers. Here, concepts of "culture" were spread through the discourse and practice of colonial slavery, with images disseminated through colonial reports.

3. For a detailed, historical analysis of the September 30th movement and the events leading to the mass killings of 1965–66, see John Roosa, *Pretext for Mass Murder: The September 30th Movement and Suharto's Coup d'état*

in Indonesia (Madison: University of Wisconsin Press, 2006). Roosa suggests the murders occurred on a date other than September 30 and argues that the majority of the leadership of the PKI was uninvolved and unaware of the action; the fabricated background of the event was meant to mislead the public into accepting the military's "pretext for mass murder" (4–18).

4. See Geoffrey Robinson, *The Dark Side of Paradise* (Ithaca, N.Y.: Cornell University Press, 1995), 273, 296–303; Baskara T. Wardaya, *Bung Karno Menggugat: Dari Marhaen, CIA, Pembantaian Massal '65 hingga G 30 S* (Yogyakarta, Indonesia: Galang Press, 2006), 63; Theodore Friend, *Indonesian Destines* (Cambridge, Mass.: Harvard University Press, 2003), 114.

5. Wardaya, *Bung Karno Menggugat,* 27–30.

6. Between 1999 and 2006, I conducted many interviews on this situation, mostly in East Java. My findings are also supported by many memoirs and research on women's oral history. Please see the section "Kisah Para Korban" (Victims' Stories) in Antonius Sumarwan, SJ, *Menyeberangi Sungai Airmata: Kisah Tragis Tapol '65 dan Upaya Rekonsiliasi* (Crossing the River of Tears: Tragic Stories of Tapol '65 and Efforts at Reconciliation (Yogyakarta, Indonesia: Kanisius, 2007), 55–199; Mia Bustam, *Dari Kamp Ke Kamp* (From Camp to Camp) (Jakarta, Indonesia: Spasi & Vihara, 2008), 150–51.

7. Saskia Wieringa, "The Birth of the New Order State in Indonesia: Sexual Politics and Nationalism," *Journal of Women's History* (March 1, 2003): 70–91.

8. Further, my findings (from interviews I conducted with Ibu Samiyatun, Ibu Sis, and Ibu Mutmainah in Malang, East Java, in 2004 and 2005, as well as my experiences growing up and visiting family in that area) indicate that many women from rural areas south of Malang, in East Java, were illiterate and were not affiliated with any officially recognized, national-level women's movements. Yet they were arrested, tortured, and obligated to report to the military offices every two weeks and were subject to continual "moral guidance" from male military officers in regard to their use of traditional attire, spousal choice, religious belonging, and even sexual desire. See also Leslie Dwyer and Degung Santikarma, "When the World Turned to Chaos: 1965 and Its Aftermath in Bali Indonesia," in *The Specter of Genocide: Mass Murder in Historical Perspective,* edited by Robert Gellately and Ben Kiernan, 289–305 (New York: Cambridge University Press, 2003). Dwyer and Santikarma interviewed many young, unmarried teenage women whose male relatives were marked as PKI and who were rounded up and brought by paramilitary patrols to government offices where most of them experienced sexual humiliation and rape. In my interview with Ms. Samiatun in East

Java, she also referred euphemistically to her obligatory visits to the local military office as the "unsafe visit."

9. Many sources discuss the issue of Gerwani as a women's political movement as well as its assumed relationship to the PKI. Please see Visal Singh, "The Upheaval in Indonesia," *China Report* 2 (1966): 17–19; Katharine E. McGregor and Vanessa Hearman, "Challenges of Political Rehabilitation in Post–New Order Indonesia: The Case of Gerwani (the Indonesian Women's Movement)," *South East Asia Research* 15, no. 3 (November 2007): 355–84; *The Indonesian Killings: Studies from Java and Bali,* Monash Papers on Southeast Asia no. 21, edited by Robert Cribb (Monash, Victoria, Australia: Monash University, Center for Southeast Asian Studies, 1990), xx. In this book I focus on how the politics of narrative relate to Gerwani as representative of new (and threatening) female alliances, and how women's bodies were so effectively transformed into collective signifiers of contemporary threats to established patriarchy.

10. Saskia Wieringa, *Sexual Politics in Indonesia* (England: Palgrave Macmillan, 2002).

11. A prime example of the "quiet" U.S. response to the massacres is shown by the rapid changes in *Time* magazine's reportage during the period following the massacres. *Time* published a number of small reports on the September 30th coup attempt and the subsequent killings, initially questioning Suharto's theory that PKI leadership was behind the coup: "Still unresolved last week was whether the six generals were martyrs slain by Communist-supported plotters. . . . Yet many an old Djakarta hand is convinced that the Reds were not the masterminds. For one thing, Untung's [the self-acknowledged leader of the coup] clumsy and ill-planned coup lacked the slick organization one would expect from efficient Communist Party Chief D. N. Aidit. With 3,500,000 members, plus his large and increasing influence on Sukarno's policies, Aidit was doing well enough as things were" ("Indonesia: Wanted: A Magician," October 15, 1965).

The illegal mass killings of unarmed, suspected PKI were also initially highlighted by *Time* in a somewhat critical way: "According to accounts brought out of Indonesia by Western diplomats and independent travelers, Communists, Red sympathizers and their families are being massacred by the thousands. Backlands army units are reported to have executed thousands of Communists after interrogation in remote rural jails . . . in Central Java the army even gave military training to Moslem youths. The murder campaign became so brazen in parts of rural East Java that Moslem bands placed the heads of victims on poles and paraded them through villages. The killings have been on such a scale that the disposal of the corpses has created a serious sanitation problem in East Java and northern Sumatra, where the humid air bears the reek of decaying flesh. Travelers from those areas tell of small rivers and streams that have been literally clogged with bodies; river transportation has at places been impeded" ("Indonesia: Silent Settlement," December 17, 1965).

Yet by mid-1966, in a much longer piece lauding Suharto's rise to power and gradual usurpation of Sukarno's leadership, *Time* had changed its tune, and the gruesome, detailed realism of earlier reports, signifying the potential violation of human—albeit "Red"—rights, had all but vanished. It was replaced with the following rather mystifyingly worded offering: "Amid a boiling bloodbath that almost unnoticed took 400,000 lives, Indonesia, the sprawling giant of Southeast Asia, has done a complete about-face. A new regime has risen, backed by the army but scrupulously constitutional and commanding vociferous popular support. 'Indonesia is a state based on law not on mere power,' says its new leader, a quietly determined Javanese general whose only name is Suharto." In this article, the September 30th movement, following Suharto and the military's discourse, is blamed on the Reds and given as just cause for Suharto's so-called smiling revenge: the "almost unnoticed" massacre of 400,000 people. "Suharto regained control of Djakarta within 24 hours, wiped out the last resistance in the Red strongholds of East and Central Java in less than six weeks. Party Boss Aidit, who was found hiding in the closet of a friend's house in Solo, was executed in a military jail and buried in an unmarked grave" ("Indonesia: Vengeance with a Smile," July 15, 1966). Throughout the article, the mention of the violence is consistently connected to the goal of fighting communism on a local as well as a global scale. Tellingly, in this context, the killings are described as having been carried out by a now-transformed citizenry led by Suharto: "Under Suharto, the nation that last year was a virtual Peking satellite has become a vigorous foe of Red China. And in an orgy of flashing knives and coughing guns, it has virtually wiped out the Partai Komunis Indonesia (P.K.I.)—which under Sukarno had grown to be the third largest Communist Party in the world."

12. One part of the significance of the event is its location in the multiethnic space of the capital, where it is made available to a general domestic (and partially foreign) audience in the national language. Thus, while in important ways the "first" such event, it does not supersede conversations about the massacres that have occurred among the members of certain ethnic groups, such as Balinese or Javanese women during specific ceremonial activities.

13. Among activists, the once-stigmatizing term *ekstapol* (an acronym

for *ex-tahanan politik* or ex–political prisoner) has more recently become something of a badge of honor.

14. Quoted in John Ochoa, "Said, Foucault, and the Desire for Analogy," in *Paradoxical Citizenship: Edward Said,* edited by Sylvia Nagy-Zekmi (Lanham, Md.: Lexington Books, 2006), 55.

15. Quoted in ibid., 55.

16. Caren Kaplan, *Questions of Travel: Postmodern Discourses of Displacement* (Durham, N.C.: Duke University Press, 1996), 98.

17. Ibid., 89.

18. Marta Savigliano includes a brilliant discussion on the issues of national identity reconstruction and its commodification in *Tango and the Political Economy of Passion* (Boulder, Colo.: Westview, 1995), 137–68.

19. Dominant bodies in the global context (global stage) will reflect differences that are further complicated by race and citizenship and immigration issues and also the global consumption of the products of the world arts industry.

20. Smadar Lavie, "Staying Put: Crossing the Palestine/Israeli Border with Gloria Anzaldúa," *Anthropology and Humanism* (June 2011): 101–21.

21. For example, certain dance practices (*Rantak, Saman, Seudati,* and others) in Aceh and Sumatra have sparked national-level interest and have been included in curricula and national competitions. The forms have also been brought to the international stage by diplomats and Indonesian students who study abroad. One of the forms, *Saman,* came from the region of Sumatra that has recently been subject to the largest presence of national security forces and a correspondingly high level of human rights abuses by soldiers in response to local independence movements. Members of the occupying military forces have reportedly also learned and publicly performed *Saman* as a method for gaining the sympathy of the local population as well as national- (and international-) level support for its "benevolent" presence there. In typical fashion, in November 2011, UNESCO gave recognition to the *Saman* form as an "intangible cultural art" with no mention whatsoever of the politicized context of the dance. This is quite typical of UNESCO's long-standing alignment with the interests and cultural policies of the Indonesian government and reveals the interconnectivity of the multiculturalism of the Indonesian state (local) with that of the international community (in this case UNESCO). See: http://www.unesco.org/culture/ich/en/USL/00509.

22. Achille Mbembe, *On the Postcolony: Studies on the History of Society and Culture* (Berkeley and Los Angeles: University of California Press, 2001), 19.

23. Indonesia gained independence from the Dutch in 1945; previously, Indonesia was known as the Dutch or Netherland East Indies. Sukarno was the first president, and Suharto came to power after the massacres in 1965.

24. Michel Foucault, *"Society Must Be Defended": Lectures at the College de France, 1975–1976,* translated by David Macey (New York: Picador, 2003), 260.

25. Achille Mbembe, "On the Postcolony: A Brief Response to Critics," *African Identities* 4, no. 2 (2006): 148.

26. Here I refer mainly to the film *Pengkhianatan G30S PKI (The Treason of the September 30th movement and the PKI),* directed by Arifin C. Noer (Jakarta, Indonesia: PPFN, 1982), which is analyzed in greater detail in chapter 2. Of similar relevance is also the *Indonesia Indah* series, three heavily ideologically freighted IMAX films commissioned by Suharto's wife around the same time as Noer's film. They continue to be screened daily at the "world's biggest" IMAX theater in Taman Mini theme park in Jakarta and were once a regular destination for the field trips of both local schoolchildren and visiting foreign dignitaries. For a more thorough analysis of the *Indonesia Indah* films, see Martin Roberts, "Indonesia: The Movie," in *Cinema and Nation,* edited by Mette Hjort and Scott Mackenzie, 173–88 (New York: Routledge, 2000).

27. Joseph Saunders, *Academic Freedom in Indonesia: Dismantling Soeharto-Era Barriers* (New York: Human Rights Watch, 1998).

28. Ibid., 2.

29. Moriana Antonio Gomez and Mercedes F. Duran-Cogan, "Introduction," in *National Identities and Sociopolitical Changes in Latin America* (New York: Routledge, 2001), xiii.

30. Gayatri Chakravorty Spivak, *A Critique of Postcolonial Reason: Toward a History of the Vanishing Present* (Cambridge, Mass.: Harvard University Press, 1999), 304.

31. Benedict Anderson, *Imagined Communities* (New York: Verso, 1991), 4.

32. Here I am inspired by Asha Vararadjan's theorization of the non-separation between the symbolic and the physical and her analysis of the material effects of the discursive in "Afterword: The Phenomenology of Violence and the Politics of Becoming," *Comparative Studies of South Asia, Africa and the Middle East* 28, no. 1 (2008): 124–41.

33. Anderson, *Imagined Communities,* 9–11.

34. *Resistance* in this context refers to the recognition of mobility as a fluid space to mediate the different conversations that can emerge on and around the "global stage."

35. My use of somatic experience here is indebted to Smadar Lavie's

theorization of issues of the body and somatic experience in response to state control in *The Poetics of Military Occupation: Mzeina Allegories of Bedouin Identity under Israeli and Egyptian Rule* (Berkeley: University of California Press, 1990).

36. Marta Elena Savigliano, "Worlding Dance and Dancing Out There in the World," in *Worlding Dance,* edited by Susan Leigh Foster, 163–87 (London: Palgrave Macmillan, 2009).

37. Ananya Chatterjea, *Butting Out: Reading Resistive Choreographies through Works by Jawole Willa Jo Zollar and Chandralekha* (Middletown, Vt.: Wesleyan University Press, 2004), 7.

38. Rustom Bharucha, "Under the Sign of Asia: Rethinking Creative Unity beyond the Rebirth of Traditional Arts," *Inter-Asia Cultural Studies* 2, no. 1 (April 2001): 151–55.

39. I use the concepts of "free trade zone" and "flexibility" with reference to Aihwa Ong, *Flexible Citizenship: The Cultural Logics of Transnationality* (Durham, N.C.: Duke University Press, 1999); and Ong, "The Gender and Labor Politics of Postmodernity," in *The Politics of Culture in the Shadow of Capital: Worlds Aligned (Post Contemporary Interventions),* edited by Lisa Lowe and David Lloyd, 89, 61–98 (Durham, N.C.: Duke University Press, 1997).

40. Wardaya, *Bung Karno Menggugat,* 63.

41. Roosa, *Pretext for Mass Murder,* 1; Audrey R. Kahin and George McT. Kahin, *Subversion as Foreign Policy: The Secret Eisenhower and Dulles Debacle in Indonesia* (New York: New Press, 1995), 1.

42. Savigliano, *Tango and the Political Economy of Passion,* 3.

43. George J. Aditjondro, "Membongkar Kleptokrasi Warisan Suharto: Mungkinkah?" (Tear Down the Kleptocratic Heritage of Suharto: A Possibility?), in *Suharto Sehat (Suharto Is Healthy),* edited by Islah Gusmian (Yogyakarta, Indonesia: Galang Press, 2006), 171–77.

44. For further information on UNESCO's policies, see the "Culture" page of UNESCO's website and the link to "Safeguarding of Intangible Cultural Heritage" under "Conventions": http://www.unesco.org/new/en/culture.

45. Edward Said, *Orientalism* (New York: Random House, 1978), 15.

46. Robinson, *The Dark Side of Paradise,* 18.

2. What Is Left

1. *Angkatan Bersenjata* (an Indonesian military newspaper), December 13, 1965, quoted in Wieringa, *Sexual Politics in Indonesia,* 314.

2. Ibid.

3. Benedict Anderson, *Imagined Communities* (New York: Verso, 1983).

4. *Pengkhianatan G-30-S PKI,* directed by Arifin C. Noer (Jakarta, Indonesia: PPFN, 1982), film. Although it became difficult to obtain copies of the film following the fall of Suharto in 1998, it is now once again easily found on the shelves of video rental stores and is posted in several parts on YouTube (http://www.youtube.com/watch?v=y6bO8gNs8mc).

5. In the film, members of Gerwani are shown dancing, orgiastically and scantily clad, with the men of the PKI and attacking, maiming, and gouging out the eyes of the seven high-ranking Army officers who were killed on September 30, 1965. While not explicitly shown in the film, their actions are obviously also meant to imply adherence to the official narrative of the September 30th Movement, in which Gerwani members allegedly danced naked while cutting off the genitalia of the officers with razor blades.

6. For further analysis of P4, see Saunders, *Academic Freedom in Indonesia,* 62.

7. Anderson, *Imagined Communities,* 187.

8. In this sense it is difficult not to marvel at the "brilliance" of Suharto's strategic takeover, detailed in chapter 1: slowly usurping the ever-popular Sukarno's hold on power after claiming to have saved him from an alleged coup d'état attempt whose shadowy perpetrators would continue to threaten the entire nation unless Suharto remained in command.

9. Wieringa, *Sexual Politics in Indonesia,* 390.

10. In *Dark Side of Paradise,* Robinson also addresses the thorough vilification of Gerwani and PKI in connection to each other: "Like the fabricated stories about Gerwani women performing a naked dance while castrating and gouging the eyes of the captured generals in Jakarta on the 1st of October, these revelations served to make PKI members appear not merely simple political traitors but as immoral, debauched, and inhuman" (293).

11. Benedict Anderson, *"Petrus Dadi Ratu," New Left Review* 3 (May–June 2000): 9.

12. Dwyer and Santikarma, "When the World Turned to Chaos," 291.

13. See Wieringa, *Sexual Politics in Indonesia.*

14. Cohen, *Performing Otherness.*

15. Ibid., 7.

16. Ibid., 9.

17. Saunders, *Academic Freedom in Indonesia,* sec. IV.

18. Much of the writing on *Bedhaya* and Javanese (and Balinese) court dance reaffirms this notion of myth and power in the relationship of the

king and the feminine figure and its practice in daily life. Western and local researchers alike have frequently been drawn in by the discourse of authenticity and history surrounding the palace arts. They are the Indonesian forms most heavily studied, written about, and frequently taught in universities and academic and performance studies contexts throughout the world; this in turn contributes greatly to cementing their importance on the national and global stage, along with the "truth" of the mythical discourse surrounding them. Among others, see Claire Holt and Rolf de Maré, *Dance Quest in Celebes* (Paris: Les Archives Internationales de la Danse, 1939); Walter Spies and Beryl de Zoete, *Dance Drama in Bali* (London: Faber and Faber, 1938); Xenia Zarina, *Classic Dances of the Orient* (New York: Crown, 1967); Jan Hostetler, "Bedhaya Semang: The Sacred Dance of Yogyakarta," *Archipelago* 24, no. 24 (1981): 127–42; Nancy H. Florida, "The Bedhaya Katawang: A Translation of the Song of Kangjeng Ratu," *Indonesia* 53 (April 1992): 20–32 (http://www.jstor.org/stable/3351112); Clara Brakel-Papenhuizen, *The Bedhaya Court Dance of Central Java* (Leiden: Brill, 1997).

19. Here my argument follows that of Martin Roberts regarding Suharto's use of touristic, travelogue films to a similar end in "Indonesia: The Movie," 173–88. Roberts argues that in the New Order era, the state-sponsored IMAX film series *Indonesia Indah (Beautiful Indonesia)* functioned as a "national identity kit" that positioned Indonesians as if they were tourists looking in at a constructed, exoticized, traditional version of "themselves."

20. Under nonritual circumstances, the sultan is normally seen in a business suit, or, during his regular games of golf near the posh Yogyakarta Hyatt hotel, in more casual attire.

21. For further analysis of *Bedhaya* and other forms in the context of the 1990 Los Angeles festival, see Barbara Kirshenblatt-Gimblett, *Destination Culture: Tourism, Museums, and Heritage* (Berkeley and Los Angeles: University of California Press, 1998), 214.

22. Justus M. Van der Kroef, "Structural Change in Indonesian Society," *Economic Development and Cultural Change* 1, no. 3 (October 1952): 216–28. This is also mentioned by Ibu Sukerni in an interview I conducted with her in 2006 in Denpasar, Bali.

23. Keith Foulcher, *Social Commitment in Literature and the Arts: The Indonesian "Institute of People's Culture," 1950–1965* (Monash, Victoria, Australia: Monash University Center for Southeast Asian Studies, 1986).

24. When compared to the Suharto years, the Sukarno era was indeed "open and varied." However, it, too, should not be idealized: in the late

1950s and early '60s Sukarno became increasingly authoritarian, suddenly dissolving Parliament and reinstating it with a majority of his own hand-picked allies and passing a decree that made him president for life. Sukarno also at times bullied and jailed political opponents, and his crackdown on Western popular culture went so far as to arrest the famous band Koes Plus for playing rock and roll in public. In addition, he was fond of making rather essentializing comments about Balinese culture, which he saw as an apt symbol to represent Indonesia internationally, although his support of such efforts was minimal in comparison to Suharto. For detailed analyses of the Sukarno era and the lead-up to 1965, see Audrey R. Kahin and George McT. Kahin, *Subversion as Foreign Policy: The Secret Eisenhower and Dulles Debacle in Indonesia* (New York: New Press, 1995); Robinson, *Dark Side of Paradise,* 273, 296–303; Wardaya, *Bung Karno Menggugat*; Roosa, *Pretext for Mass Murder*; Daniel S. Lev, "Indonesia 1965: The Year of the Coup," *Asian Survey* 6, no. 2 (February 1966): 103–10; Benedict R. O'G. Anderson, "Introduction," in *Violence and the State's Suharto's Indonesia* (Ithaca, N.Y.: Cornell Southeast Asia Program Publications, 2001), 9–20. In terms of the variation and openness to more diverse genres in cultural missions or literature exchange, translation, and adaptation in the Soekarno era, I also refer to Jennifer Lindsay and Maya H. T. Liem (eds.), *Heirs to World Culture: Being Indonesian 1950–1965* (Leiden: KITLV Press, 2012).

25. For more on Dardanella, see Ramadhan Karta Hadimadja, *Gelombang Hidupku: Dewi Dja Dari Dardanella* (Jakarta, Indonesia: Sinar Harapan, 1982); Matthew Isaac Cohen, *Komedie Stamboel: Popular Theater in Colonial Indonesia, 1891–1903* (Columbus: Ohio State University Press, 2006), 335–68.

26. Hadimadja, *Gelombang Hidupku.*

27. Cohen, *Komedie Stamboel,* 335–68.

28. For a detailed analysis of cultural policy and changes in cultural policy during the Sukarno years, see Tod Jones, *Indonesian Cultural Policy 1950–2003: Culture, Institutions, Government,* unpublished doctoral dissertation, Perth, Australia: Curtin University of Technology, Department of Media and Information, November 2005). See also Daniel S. Lev, *The Transition to Guided Democracy: Indonesian Politics 1957–1959* (Ithaca, N.Y.: Cornell Modern Indonesia Project Monograph Series, 1966).

29. Theodore Friend, *Indonesian Destinies* (Cambridge, Mass.: Harvard University Press, 2003), 104. For further analysis of Indonesia's relationship to China during Sukarno see Sen-Yu Dai, "Peking's International Position and the Cold War," *Annals of the American Academy of Political and Social*

Science 321, no. 1 (January 1959): 117–20. For more information on the United States' actions and policies resulting from apprehensions over the spread of communism in Southeast Asia in the 1950s and '60s, see Kahin and Kahin, *Subversion as Foreign Policy;* Noam Chomsky, *Rethinking Camelot: JFK, the Vietnam War, and the U.S. Political Culture* (Cambridge, Mass.: South End Press, 1999), 48; and others.

30. See Robinson, *Dark Side of Paradise;* Wardaya, *Bung Karno Menggugat;* and Kahin and Kahin, *Subversion as Foreign Policy;* Anderson, *Violence and the State's Suharto's Indonesia;* Lev, "Indonesia 1965," and others.

31. Robinson, *Dark Side of Paradise,* 304.

32. Partha Chatterjee, *Nationalist Thought and the Colonial World* (Minneapolis: University of Minnesota Press, 1998).

33. The song was labeled a communist anthem and banned by the New Order state, despite its rather innocuous lyrics idealizing a leafy vegetable of the same name: *Genjer* is a type of water spinach with a flower (in Latin the flower is *Limnocharis flava,* commonly called Yellow Burrhead in English) that was a popular crop and side dish in Indonesia prior to 1965. The main lyrics are a rather humdrum description of farming: *"Njer genjer ring kedhokan pating keleler mak e thole teka-teka mbubuti genjer ole satenong mengko sedhot sing thole-thole genjer genjer saiki digawa mole"* (Genjer-Genjer spread on the field, the mother of my son [Javanese way to refer to a wife] soon after her arrival picking the Genjer, after she gets one basket she brings it home). This flower has a significant value especially for economically less well-off people in Java, because during the Second World War and continuing until today, it often replaces the function of rice when the price of rice is very high. Flowers are also commonly associated with women and are often used to describe seduction. Genjer, however, is also considered a weed that many Javanese believe needs to be removed in order to make rice grow properly. In the song itself, Genjer as a vegetable was treated equally with rice, to be presented on the table as food for a family, perhaps giving it a "proletarian" slant. The main reason, however, for its banning by the New Order was more likely its widespread popularity and effective use at political rallies prior to 1965, particularly, but not exclusively, those of the left. See Francisca Ria Susanti, *Kembang Kembang Genjer* (Jakarta, Indonesia: Lembaga Sastra Pembebasan, 2006).

34. Interview with Ibu Sis in Malang, East Java, 2000.

35. The legal amendment MPRS no. XXV, 1966, affected many people, but especially those suspected of having connections to the Communist Party. Based on this amendment, the Ministry of Internal Affairs instituted

a rule that no citizenship identity card (*Kartu Tanda Penduduk* or KTP) would be issued to those who had had any sort of "ties"—whether direct or even through a distant relative—to the PKI at any time in the course of their lives. The KTP is required for certain legal processes regarding education and citizenship; this amendment excluded even family members of accused communists from these basic rights. It also excluded most Gerwani members and some female artists who had merely been hired to perform for Gerwani or other left-leaning political events. For example, one dancer has been refused a KTP from 1965 until the present simply because she was known to have performed at a single PKI celebration in June 1965 (Ibu Sariatun, personal interview, Malang, East Java, 2000). For further analysis of the effects of official *Ekstapol* status, see Wieringa, *Sexual Politics in Indonesia*, 4; and Justus M. van der Kroef, "Indonesia's Political Prisoners," *Pacific Affairs* 49, no. 4 (Winter 1976–77): 625–47.

36. Anderson, *Imagined Communities,* 206.

3. Historicizing Violence

1. Macarena Gómez-Barris, *Where Memory Dwells: Culture and State Violence in Chile* (Berkeley and Los Angeles: University of California Press, 2009).

2. Assia Djebar, *Fantasia, an Algerian Cavalcade,* translated by Dorothy Blair (New York: Quartet, 1989).

3. This distinction was instituted and practiced in the everyday context of school during my childhood. While in the past, few Western scholars have tried to raise complicated, critical questions about the standardized dichotomy of *halus* and *kasar* and have tended to contribute to its continuing canonization (see, for example, Bernard Arp [ed.], *Performance in Java and Bali: Study of Narrative, Theatre, Music and Dance* [London: School of Oriental and African Studies, 1993], 52–71; Henry Spiller, *Erotic Triangles: Sudanese Dance and Masculinity in West Java* [Chicago: University of Chicago Press, 2010]; Karl G. Heider, *Landscapes of Emotion: Mapping of Three Cultures of Indonesia* [New York: Cambridge University Press, 1991]), I must note that much exemplary, detailed research by foreign scholars has emerged in recent years. Among others are the work of Matthew Cohen and Felicia Hughes-Freeland, who pay close attention to Javanese arts and its sociopolitical categorization of taste and commodification. See, for example, Cohen's two books (*Komedie Stramboel* and *Performing Otherness*) and Felicia Hughes-Freeland, "Art and Politics: From Javanese Court Dance to

Indonesian Art," *Journal of the Royal Anthropological Institute* 3, no. 3 (September 1997): 475–93.

4. Interview with Bondan Nusantara, a cultural activist in Yogyakarta, August 14, 2006; interview with Dr. Lono Simatupang, professor of anthropology, Gadjah Mada University, Yogyakarta, Central Java, Indonesia, August 10, 2006; interview with Dr. Sumandyo Hadi, professor of performance studies, Institute of the Arts, Yogyakarta, Central Java, Indonesia, August 20, 2006. For more information on *Jathilan,* see also Ward Keeler, "Villagers and the Exemplary Center in Java," *Indonesia* 39 (April 1985): 111–40; Kevin O. Browne, "Awareness, Emptiness, and Javanese Selves: *Jathilan* Performance in Yogyakarta, Indonesia," *Asia Pacific Journal of Anthropology* 4, nos. 1&2 (2003): 54–71.

I also attended many performances of *Jathilan* and *Jaranan* (the East Javanese version) during my childhood in Java and have continued to do so until the present.

5. See Robert W. Hefner, "The Politics of Popular Art: *Tayuban* Dance and Culture Change in East Java," *Indonesia* 43 (April 1987): 75–94; Ben Suharto, *Tayub, Pengamatan dari Segi Tari Pergaulan serta Kaitannya dengan Unsur Upacara Kesuburan* (Tayub: Survey of a Social Dance and Its Relation to Elements of Fertility Ceremonies) (Yogyakarta: Akademi Seni Tari Indonesia, 1980); Clifford Geertz, *The Religion of Java* (New York: Free Press, 1960), 300.

6. For a detailed discussion of these events (the happenings in my grandmother's yard and the PKK meetings around Independence Day) in specific relation to the concept of neoliberalism, see my chapter, "Desiring the Stage: The Interplay of Mobility and Resistance," in *Neoliberalism and Global Theaters,* edited by Lara D. Nielsen and Patricia Ybarra (London: Palgrave Macmillan, 2012), 256–65.

7. M. Jacqui Alexander, "Erotic Autonomy as a Politics of Decolonization: An Anatomy of Feminist and State Practice in the Bahamas Tourist Economy," in *Feminist Genealogies, Colonial Legacies, Democratic Futures,* edited by Alexander and Chandra Talpade Mohanty (New York: Routledge, 1997), 65.

8. Interview with Siti Samidjah, August 16, 1991, Malang, East Java, Indonesia. I also refer to Mari Condro Negoro's analysis of Dutch influence in Javanese culture, in *Busana Adat Keraton Yogyakarta, 1877–1937* (The Traditional Costume of the Yogyakarta Palace, 1877–1937) (Yogyakarta, Indonesia: Yayasan Pustaka Nusatama, 1995). See also Ann Laura Stoller, *Carnal Knowledge and Imperial Power: Race and the Intimate in Colonial Rule* (Berkeley and Los Angeles: University of California Press, 2002). Further, as men-

tioned in chapter 1, particularly in terms of Javanese court dance, foreign influence was often a "welcome" catalyst for change. In the mid-colonial period, it frequently inspired the rethinking and reornamentation of various forms by master choreographers from the palace, partially in response to the demand for performances in Europe and the potential for mobility this offered. For more on Javanese and Balinese court dance during colonialism, see Cohen, *Performing Otherness.*

9. Despite having submitted several official letters of resignation over the past decade, the response has always been that my requests are "being processed" and subject to further review by the myriad levels of government bureaucratic structure. The difficulty of extricating oneself from the much-idealized "end" of serving the Indonesian government (a state of affairs in which one's complex dependence on an organization indeed renders one's aesthetic knowledge and related historical memories as collectively administered "intellectual property") is one of the many, ill-portending carryovers from the Suharto years to the present era of *Reformasi.*

10. See Hiski Darmayana, "Tari Gandrung: Seni Perlawanan Wong Osing" (Gandrung Dance: Art of the Struggle of the Osing People), *Osingkertarajasa.com* (December 2011), at http://osingkertarajasa.wordpress .com/tari-gandrung-seni-perlawanan-wong-osing/; James L. Peacock, *Rites of Modernization: Symbolic and Social Aspects of Indonesian Proletarian Drama (Symbolic Anthropology)* (Chicago: University of Chicago Press, 1987).

11. The detailed information on the experience of 1965–66 in Banyuwangi comes from interviews I conducted with Mohammad Toha (2000), the son of a prominent local *kiai,* or religious teacher and leader. I also conducted interviews with former dancers from Banyuwangi (2000) and members (Khusnul, Nurul) of the Yogyakarta activist group Syarikat Indonesia (2005) who had collected oral histories of 1965 and its aftermath in Banyuwangi and other parts of East Java.

12. Leslie Dwyer, "The Intimacy of Terror: Gender and the Violence of 1965–66 in Bali," *Intersections: Gender, History and Culture in the Asian Context* 10 (August 2004), at http://www.sshe.murdoch.edu.au/intersections/ issue10/dwyer.html.

13. Interview with Siti Samidjah. See also Hiski Darmayana, "Tari Gandrung."

14. The liner notes for *Songs before Dawn: Gandrung Banyuwangi* (the first CD in Smithsonian Folkways' extensive *Music of Indonesia* series) can be downloaded free of charge from the Smithsonian website at http:// www.folkways.si.edu/albumdetails.aspx?itemid=2270. Written by Philip Yampolsky, an experienced ethnomusicologist and musician and the series

editor, the notes provide detailed and informative technical and social descriptions of several *Gandrung* performances. See also Philip Yampolsky, "Forces for Change in the Regional Performing Arts of Indonesia," *Bijdragen tot de Taal-, Land- en Volkenkunde* 151, 4de Afl., *Performing Arts in Southeast Asia* (1995): 700–25.

15. Interview with Ibu Kabul (a former dancer from Central Java who was accused of membership in Lekra and imprisoned for over a decade in 1965), Jakarta, 2004. See also Choirotun Chisaan, "In Search of Islamic Cultural Identity," in Lindsay and Liem, *Heirs to World Culture.*

16. See "The Impact of Intellectual Property Laws on Indonesian Traditional Arts," a 2005 report by the Indonesian Media Law and Policy Centre in cooperation with the Social Science Research Council and Ford Foundation, available at http://mediaresearchhub.ssrc.org.

17. Ibid.

18. Walter Benjamin, "The Work of Art in the Age of Mechanical Reproduction" (orig. 1935), in *Illuminations,* edited by Hannah Arendt, translated by Harry Zohn (New York: Schocken, 1968), II, 217–52.

19. Ibid., II.

20. Ibid., II.

21. John Pemberton, *On the Subject of "Java"* (Ithaca, N.Y.: Cornell University Press, 1994), 10–11.

22. See Antonio Gramsci, "Hegemony," in *Cultural Theory and Popular Culture,* edited by John Storey (Athens: University of Georgia Press, 1998), 210–16.

23. See chapter 2 for a detailed analysis of *Bedhaya* and its central position within the realm of nationalized royal arts.

24. During the colonial era, kings and other royalty also generally performed a co-opted, figurehead role that served to symbolically legitimize the authority of the Dutch in the eyes of the general populace.

25. Said, *Orientalism,* 32–34.

26. Jean Baudrillard, *Simulacra and Simulation,* translated by Sheila Faria Glaser (Ann Arbor: University of Michigan Press, 1994), 6.

27. Bharucha, "Under the Sign of Asia," 151.

28. Savigliano, *Tango and the Political Economy of Passion,* 32.

29. See chapter 5 for a further analysis and explanation of my use of this term and its politics in relation to the Western-led international community.

30. Anna Lowenhaupt Tsing, *In the Realm of the Diamond Queen: Marginality in an Out-of-the-Way Place* (Princeton, N.J.: Princeton University Press, 1993), 5.

4. Staging Alliances

1. *Front Uni National pour un Cambodge Indépendant, Neutre, Pacifique, et Coopératif* (Royal political party, founded by King Norodhom Sihanouk).

2. King Sisowath is a half-brother of King Sihanouk. For a detailed analysis of the lineages and historical tensions between them, see Milton E. Osborne, *Sihanouk: Prince of Light, Prince of Darkness* (Honolulu: University of Hawaii Press, 2004). For a comparative analysis of Cambodia's international positioning in the context of Cold War political relations between southeast nations and the West, see also Kahin and Kahin, *Subversion as Foreign Policy.*

3. In the Royal University of Fine Arts, the dance department is divided into two major styles: classical Cambodian dance and folk dance. Cambodian state troupes touring abroad on official culture missions mostly perform Cambodian classical dance. But this year, 2002, Cambodian folk dance had begun to be performed for official events both inside and outside of the country. The folk dances mainly describe rural scenes: the lives of fishermen, rice harvests, forestry, and village youth and workers are portrayed by students from the Royal University of Fine Arts.

4. Amitav Ghosh, *Dancing in Cambodia, at Large in Burma* (New Delhi: Ravi Dayal, 1998), 3–4.

5. This relationship is explained in more detail in the preface.

6. I interviewed Innayatulah in Aceh (the local area hardest hit by the 2004 tsunami), January 2012. She indicated that the flood of international relief following the tsunami had been helpful, but it failed to address the ongoing political violence and clashes between government forces and local resistance fighters that, for many, have long constituted a far more urgent source of trauma. For an analysis of the changing politics of terms like *trauma* and *crisis* in Indonesia in the context of recent natural disasters and the long-term effects of state violence, see Leslie Dwyer and Degung Santikarma, "Posttraumatic Politics: Violence, Memory, and Biomedical Discourse in Bali," in *Understanding Trauma: Integrating Biological, Clinical, and Cultural Perspectives,* edited by Laurence D. Kirmayer, Robert Lemelson, and Mark Barad (Cambridge, England: Cambridge University Press, 2007), 403–32. See also Jonathan Zilberg, "The Achenese Museum Conflict: Does Aceh Really Need a US$7.5 Million Tsunami Museum," *Komunitas Tikar Pandan,* April 2008.

7. Interview with Ibu Saritun, Malang, East Java, August 2000. I also refer to an interview with Ibu Tas Katias, Malang, East Java, 2001.

8. Interviews with Ibu Sukerni, Denpasar, Bali, 2002, and Ibu Mayun,

Denpasar, Bali, 2007. I also refer to analyses of the killings by neighbors and local officials who joined militias in Bali, as well as the specific effects on women suspected of involvement with the PKI, in Dwyer, "The Intimacy of Terror." See also Dwyer and Santikarma, "When the World Turned to Chaos," 289–305; and Robinson, *Dark Side of Paradise.*

9. Interview with Ibu Sukerni, Denpasar, Bali, 2004; conversation with Degung Santikarma and Ibu Mayun, Denpasar, Bali, 2006.

10. On several occasions (June 2007; July 2008; July 2009; July 2010), I have conducted interviews with members of this *Barong* dance venue, including the director, senior dancers and choreographer, and musicians, as well as with tourists attending the shows. The interviews were conducted together with activist members of the local community, who have also founded and built a space (in which they hold discussions, concerts, art exhibitions, and other events) to commemorate the violence in 1965–66. The space is called *Taman 65,* or "65 Park," and has the numerals "1965" inlaid in stone in the center of its main space in Kesiman, Denpasar, Bali. The space has a website at http://taman65.wordpress.com/.

11. See Wieringa, *Sexual Politics in Indonesia;* Dwyer, "The Intimacy of Terror"; Dwyer and Santikarma, "When the World Turned to Chaos"; Robinson, *Dark Side of Paradise;* and the film, *40 Years of Silence: An Indonesian Tragedy,* directed by Robert Lemelson (Boston: Documentary Educational Resources, 2009), DVD, which contains interviews with Balinese survivors of the 1965–66 killings.

12. Interview with Ibu Ketut Pandriya, Denpasar, Bali, March 2005.

5. Violence and Mobility

1. Mbembe, *On the Postcolony,* 7.

2. United Nation's Transitional Authority in Cambodia, 1993.

3. Dharma Wanita is the association of civil servants' wives. A member's rank is based on her husband's position in his respective division of the governmental structure. For example, the wife of the head officer will be the head of Dharma Wanita at that office and in that particular department. Thus, the wife of the Indonesian ambassador in Cambodia was automatically the head of Dharma Wanita in Cambodia. Her staff consisted of the wives of all the vice ambassadors, such as the defense consul or economic consul, including the cultural attaché. Female civil servants are also often members of Dharma Wanita, although they are under less obligation to join than the wives; at the time of my presence in Cambodia, the cultural attaché was a single female civil servant, and consequently she served both

functions (that of diplomatic representative and mediator of cultural events for Dharma Wanita).

4. Many dancers who work at Indonesian government institutions as professor or lecturer automatically possess two positions, or *jabatan,* known as *jabatan struktural* (structural) and *jabatan fungsional* (functional). This system allows civil servants to define their attachments through the government and determines their obligations and salaries. Most civil servants are given the "blue passport"—a passport that recognizes the person who obtains it as a government officer—for use on travel abroad; within ASEAN this passport is recognized as official, and the carrier often receives different treatment from the immigration officer, such as a special entrance and a waiver of Indonesia's exit tax (the usual amount is one million rupiah—approximately US$100—to leave the country). However, this type of passport does not mean anything when entering the United States; only the position of diplomat holds any political or economic value there for Indonesians, particularly after September 11, 2001.

5. This refers to Savigliano, *Tango and the Political Economy of Passion;* Mbembe, "On the Postcolony," 149.

6. Gayatri Chakravorty Spivak, "Inscriptions: Of Truth to Size," in *Outside in the Teaching Machine* (New York: Routledge, 1993), 214.

7. Savigliano, *Tango;* Naima Prevots, *Dance for Export: Cultural Diplomacy and the Cold War* (Middletown, Vt.: Wesleyan University Press, 2001), 12. In my research, cultural diplomacy, for example, is a significant part of state-to-state interaction between Indonesia and the United States, heavily connected to trade and foreign aid agreements between the two governments. Indonesia in particular produces culture as export. As Prevots suggests, dance has taken on an important role in foreign policy and diplomacy between the West and Third World countries.

8. Fawzia Afzal Khan, "Exposed by Pakistani Street Theatre: The Unholy Alliance of Postmodern Capitalism, Patriarchy, and Fundamentalism," *Social Text* 69 (December 2001): 67–91.

9. I wondered if this embodied discipline could serve to demonstrate Foucault's theorization of punishment, in which women are located differently within the state system of rights; Anderson, *Imagined Communities,* also points out that while the nation is an "imagined" community, the actuality of power distributes its physical effects through systematic punishment that I feel as very real.

10. Interview with Maimunah and Siti from Central Java in Taiwan, 2012; also see Anne Loveband, "Positioning the Product: Indonesian Migrant Women Workers in Taiwan," *Journal of Contemporary Asia* 34, no. 3

(2007): 336–48; A. Rita Dharani, *Perlindungan Hukum Bagi Buruh Migran Dalam United Nations Convention against Transnational Organized Crime dan Realitas Perdagangan Perempuan Dalam Proses Penempatan TKW Indonesia,* unpublished master's thesis (Yogyakarta, Indonesia: Gadjah Mada University, 2005).

11. Saraswati Sunindyo, "Murder, Gender, and the Media: Sexualizing Politics and Violence," in *Fantasizing the Feminine in Indonesia,* edited by Laurie Jo Sears (Durham, N.C.: Duke University Press, 1996), 124.

12. The "state" here reveals itself as a massive, multi-tiered behemoth: female practitioners must prove they have permission to travel by carrying official documents signed by a husband or male representative *and* by officials at several different levels of administration, from the head of the village up to an officer of the central government; each signature requires a visit to a separate area, a waiting period, and often "polite" conversation, during which the exercise of state power and the pervasive resistance to the concept of women as actual, mobilized agents seems particularly tangible.

13. For example, in 2009 there were a number of arrests of female dancers who were performing at a karaoke bar because the owner of the club failed to pay "contributions" to the police and the city council on public security in West Java. The arrests did not involve the owner but rather the dancers and the low-ranking security staff of the club.

14. Dharma Wanita, the organization of the wives of civil servants, regulates women's participation in state and cultural affairs according to a center–periphery model, mirroring the militaristic structure of control employed by the Indonesian government itself. See Julia L. Suryakusuma, *Sex, Power and Nation: An Anthology of Writings, 1979–2003* (Jakarta, Indonesia: Metafor, 2004), 99.

15. I am marking specific alliances that are created in attempts at producing resistive projects. While many men and women have been performing extensively and collaborating with artists from outside of Indonesia, that does not necessarily confine the locally resistive nature of the work; it also does not free such projects from the state's mediation in terms of context and content.

16. Aihwa Ong, *Flexible Citizenship: The Cultural Logics of Transnationality* (Durham, N.C.: Duke University Press, 1999).

17. Jennifer Lindsay, "Foreword" *(kata pengantar), Jurnal Perempuan: The Journal of Women in Indonesia* 62 (Special edition 2009): 1–5.

18. Many of my former colleagues who perform and teach palace arts began their training at a very young age and were inducted into the palace

troupe based on their family's genealogical status as "royalty" who are allowed to live and own property within the palace walls in Yogyakarta or Solo.

19. Ong, *Flexible Citizenship*.

20. The notion of the global diplomatic stage as a free-trade zone that is also, paradoxically, "duty free" is also relevant for my analysis. In the particular space of convergence created by the performance of a state diplomatic culture mission abroad, the national duties of each participant—foreign diplomats, officials of the host state, dancers, possibly even presidents or prime ministers—are, in the moment of performance, temporarily "suspended" in the illusory, peaceful atmosphere of the universal appreciation of beauty in culture and art. Yet of course these very duties, and the fact that they are necessarily connected to national self-interest and not global good will, constitute the conditions of possibility for the event itself and the freeness of the space it occupies. People are there in an ideological gesture of friendship that in reality is generally motivated by base national interest and, whether direct or indirect, global political and economic competition. The performance of "culture" thus serves as the art or artifice that brings an air of pleasure and camaraderie to a meeting that in most instances is driven by the aggression and mutual mistrust that lies under the surface of relations between even the most allied of nations. Likewise, when purchasing duty-free goods in a special trade zone such as an airport, the privilege and pleasure of luxury products with no national sales tax is belied by the function of the space itself as one step closer to the naked realities of aggression and exploitation on the transnational battlefield of global capitalism.

21. Randy Martin, *Critical Moves: Dance Studies in Theory and Politics* (Durham, N.C.: Duke University Press, 1998), 4–5.

22. *Gandrung* is a "folk" form particular to East Java, which I was taught in secret by my grandmother, and later, after its reclamation and nationalization by the state, performed as a civil servant on diplomatic culture missions. See chapter 3 for an extensive analysis of the form, its subforms, and their troubled history following the rise of Suharto.

23. Jean-Luc Nancy, "Consecration and Massacres," translated by Amanda McDonald, *Post Colonial Studies* 6, no. 1 (2003): 47–53.

24. See chapter 1 for a description and analysis of this event, which took place in Jakarta in 2005.

25. Quoted in Robert Gellately and Ben Kiernan, "The Study of Mass Murder and Genocide," in *Specter of Genocide,* 15.

26. Ibid., 46–47.

27. See Robinson, *Dark Side of Paradise,* 273, 296–303; Wardaya, *Bung Karno Menggugat,* 63; Friend, *Indonesian Destinies,* 114; Cribb, ed., *Indonesian Killings,* xx; and others.

28. Gellately and Kiernan, *Specter of Genocide,* 17. Gellately and Kiernan, while still arguing that the political nature of the 1965–66 killings in Indonesia prevents them from categorization under the UN-based, "legal" definition of genocide, state that a political component to the definition of a targeted group "perhaps . . . should be" added to the legal definition (19). Their argument that mass murders under Pol Pot in Cambodia (in which, like Indonesia, the targeted "group" was forcibly defined by their killers for a number of reasons, including both ideological "impurity" and "foreign" ethnic or citizenship status) would appear to belie any claims about the legal status of the killings in Indonesia. See also Edward Kissi, "Genocide in Cambodia and Ethiopia," in Gellately and Kiernan, *Specter of Genocide,* 307–21.

INDEX

Rachmi Diyah Larasati is assistant professor of cultural theory, critical studies, and dance history in the Department of Theatre Arts and Dance at the University of Minnesota, where she holds an affiliate position in the Department of Gender, Women, and Sexuality Studies.